D-DAY PARATROOPERS

THE AMERICANS

Christophe DESCHODT,
Laurent ROUGER

Computer graphics by Jean-Marie MONGIN, André JOUINEAU, Nicolas Gohin, Yann-Erwin ROBERT and Denis GANDILHON

Translated from the French by Alan McKay and Philippe Charbonnier

HISTOIRE & COLLECTIONS - PARIS

6 June 1944,
the first encounters between American airborne troops and the French. Here, two
paratroopers are talking to a gendarme and a member of the local resistance.
(Reconstruction, photograph by Pierre Schubert)

Design and lay-out by Yann-Erwin ROBERT and Denis GANDILHON © *Histoire & Collections* 2004

All rights reserved. No part of this publication can be transmitted or reproduced without the written of the Author and the Publisher.

ISBN: 2-915239-29-0

Publisher's number: 2-915239

© Histoire & Collections 2004

A book published by
HISTOIRE & COLLECTIONS
SA au capital de 182 938, 82 €

5, avenue de la Republique
F-75541 Paris Cedex 11 France
Telephone (33-1) 40 21 18 20
Fax (33-1) 47 00 51 11

This book has been designed, typed, laid-out and processed by the Studio A&C, fully on integrated computer equipment

Printed by Zure, Spain, European Union.
September 2004

CONTENTS

'LEST WE FORGET THEM'	4
1 - THE AMERICAN AIRBORNE DIVISIONS	7
2 - THE IXth TROOP CARRIER COMMAND	16
3 - OPERATION 'NEPTUNE'	27
4 - THE JUMP SUIT	37
5 - THE STEEL HELMET	50
6 - THE T-5 PARACHUTE	62
7 - THE GLIDER-BORNE TROOPS	69
8 - WEAPONS	76
9 - EQUIPMENT	92
10 - INSIGNIA AND DECORATIONS	103
11 - THE AIRBORNE DIVISION MOTOR TRANSPORT	117
APPENDICES	124
BIBLIOGRAPHY	128

Advice to collectors

The artifacts shown in this study come from private collections or from museums and are the fruit of many years' research involving a lot of tenacity and discrimination. Such an example are the reinforced jump suits, because the few which have survived the battle are now extremely rare. Only the two airborne divisions committed in Normandy were issued with this type of uniform.

Upon their return to England, at the end of July 1944, two months later, the paratroopers were fitted out with the new M–1943 combat uniform, which was typical of operations in Holland (September 1944). The 1942 uniforms had already sunk into oblivion. Those which did survive had often deteriorated considerably; many of them were too grimy to be reused and were burnt. The reinforced jump suits that had been left on the battlefield for various reasons were often worn threadbare by farmers who were short of everything in the immediate post-war period.

One therefore has to be very careful when getting hold of a reinforced uniform these days. Any 'basic' jump suit can very quickly become one of those legendary reinforced uniforms if roughed up, camouflaged with paint, given a fake anti-gas impregnation, and even marked with a spurious army serial number or name, and then sell for a ridiculous price.

Where helmets are concerned, especially the M2, these are just as rare; the very fragile chinstrap D-ring which broke very quickly got them thrown on the scrap heap. Authentic, intact helmets are extremely rare and there are a lot of fakes around. One should check for clues of welding traces where the former rectangular loop had been before the faker soldered a more-desirable D-ring.

The majority of the authentic helmets have broken D-rings that have been crudely repaired: thick welding, substitute rings, etc. All of which leaves the field wide open for the fakers. One must also look very closely at the stitching on the chinstraps, the texture and the color of the strap.

So there are a great number of fake helmets. Beware of M1 helmets with fixed-bail loops on which authentic paratrooper MIC chinstraps (brass press studs) have been attached. As for helmets with painted insignia, one should really only trust in a sixth sense, and even then…, or hunt around the battlefield (but beware of fakes planted in local junk shops and flea markets). The paratrooper craze has also motivated a surge in spray-painted camouflaged web gear, pseudo 'rigger-made' pouches and bags, as well as heavily taped-over M-1936 suspenders. Nothing can replace handling and looking closely at authentic items in order to sharpen one's knowledge.

But our aim here is not to scare collectors but to encourage them to be more careful before investing their (hard-earned) money in buying these testimonies to the tragic and exciting lore of the American Airborne troops in Normandy.

FOREWORD

Sixty years ago during the night of 5 to 6 June 1944, 10,000 men belonging to the American Airborne forces dropped by parachute or landed by glider on Norman soil. As the vanguard of the Allied forces, they were the first to take part in the liberation of France. Many of them were killed or wounded right from the start of D-Day;
many of them were scarcely twenty-years old.
This study describing their uniforms, insignia and equipment, is intended to be a quiet tribute to those who gave their lives freely in order to liberate a country most of them had never seen.

Lest we forget them!

The historical and strategic aspects of Operation 'Neptune' are only touched on here in a general manner. A number of other books discuss the subject. A chapter has been given over to air transport and indeed, the C-47s and their crews directly involved in this fantastic adventure do have a place in this book.

For Damien, Edouard, Julien and Hadrien

Opposite page.
Lt. Kelso Horne of 1st Platoon, Item Company/508th PIR, 82d Airborne Division, was photographed at Saint-Sauveur le Vicomte on 16 June. Although he was an officer, few details distinguish him from an enlisted man. Worn slightly askew, the M2 helmet reveals a knit cap underneath. The small mesh camouflage netting has been garnished with British green and brown strips of jute. The helmet shell chinstraps have been hooked up in the netting, a very common practice. The 48-star flag has been sewn on the right-hand sleeve, whose additional elbow patch can be seen. Filled to bursting, the trousers cargo pockets are fastened down with straps. Horne has preferred the M1 rifle to the carbine normally issued to officers. A fragmentation grenade and a Colt pistol complete his armament. Slipped under the left shoulder strap, one can see the brass whistle chain, itself placed in a breast pocket. The canteen, as often with the paratroopers, is carried in a mounted troops-type cover. While the officer is posing as a 'liberator' at the request of the photographer, his look is nonetheless that of exhaustion: a haggard stare, stubble on the chin, and crumpled clothes.

CHAPTER 1 THE AMERICAN AIRBORNE DIVISION ORDER OF BATTLE

Previous airborne operations in the Mediterranean in 1943 had proved that the strength of the parachute infantry component of the airborne division, as defined by T/O 71 of 15 October 1942, was inadequate. Despite the reluctance shown by the Army high command, Major-General M.B. Ridgway, commanding officer of the 82nd Airborne Division during the Sicily landings, insisted on modifying the division's organization for the Invasion of France in the spring of 1944.

Although a new organizational table was brought out in February 1944, there was no official document to ratify the important modifications which were made between then and 6 June 1944. For D-day, the US Airborne division therefore had 3 parachute infantry regiments (PIR) instead of 1 (two being mere attachments) and the glider-borne infantry was reduced to a single regiment (reinforced by a third additional attached battalion, however) instead of two.

The manpower increase in the parachute infantry was considerable since instead of the 1,954 men planned there were no fewer than 5,862 paratroopers in each division taking part in Normandy during the night of 6 June 1944.

The 82nd and 101st Airborne Divisions' order of battle had been tailored for the occasion, this makeshift organization was not confirmed later and other changes took place in subsequent campaigns.

Above.
5 June 1944 in the evening. General Eisenhower, hiding his worries behind a thin smile, talks freely with men of the 502nd PIR on Newbury airfield (Berkshire).
"And you, soldier, what will you do when the war is over?"
"For the moment, sir, I want nothing else than get back home to Georgia and eat chickpeas and vegetables." The laughter was widespread among the soldiers who were in top condition.
"Don't you worry about anything, boss, as long as the 101st is there, all'll go well." A big lad with his face painted as black as coal even went so far as to pat the General on the back: *"After the war, if you're out of work, come and see me on my ranch in Texas, there'll be job for you!"*
The paratrooper standing at attention has a spoon - the only regulation eating utensil carried - in the side pocket of the M-1936 bag.
(National Archives)

Previous page.
Our reconstruction of Lieutenant Horne, page 5.

The Organizational Tables

Shown on pages 8 and 9, these tables shed very interesting light on the weapons, equipment and means of transport and communication.

Unlike the airborne infantry, the various arms and support services hardly changed and maintained their strength and the equipment mentioned in the 24 February 1944 Table of organization.

Even if it is not a proud mustang, this good old nag is not an unfamiliar steed to these boys from Arkansas or Texas. As the 1944 photos often show, a good number of American soldiers did not hesitate to ride these sturdy farm horses, or even horses captured from the enemy.
(Reconstruction)

GENESIS AND EVOLUTION OF THE AIRBORNE UNITS

"OK, let's go"

On Monday 5 June at 4.15, General Eisenhower confirmed his decision at a final staff meeting: D-Day would be the 6th June.

Never before in military history had a general given an order which had such consequences. On the evening of the same day, 'Ike' informally inspected some of the troops which were going to drop from the sky and face the German Army, still formidable in spite of the setbacks it had suffered. A long distance had been covered since the heroic days in 1941 when the US Army tried desperately to catch up with the Fallschirmjäger.

It was indeed the spectacular successes of the German paratroops during the 1940 battles which were at the origin of the creation of the Airborne troops. Although it was not yet in the war, the American military foresaw that their country would be entering the fray sooner or later; under the impetus of an intrepid and energetic officer, Major-General W.C. 'Bill' Lee, called the father of US paratroopers, a parachute test platoon was activated at Fort Benning (Georgia) in July 1940. In 1941 after the first promising results, the first airborne unit, the 501st Parachute Battalion, was created with 500 officers and men.

With the influx of volunteers, regiments were formed and were given a number in the 500 series.

Unlike the German and French paratroopers of the time who were part of the Air Force, these regiments were attached to the army and used its terminology. The first two American Airborne Divisions, the 82nd and the 101st were indeed originally infantry divisions which were designated 'Airborne' (A/B) in August 1942.

In November of the same year, during the Allied landings in North Africa, American airborne troops made their first combat jump, over Oran (503rd PIR, Lieutenant-Colonel Edson Raff). In July 1943, the 82nd 'All American' Division was operational and took part in the Sicily and Italy landings. But although they were important, these operations

THE AIRBORNE DIVISION (February 1944 table of organization)

STRENGTH

	Division HQ	Div HQ Co.	MP Platoon	Division Artillery	Parachute Infantry Regiment [1]	2 Glider Infantry Regiment [2]	Engineer Battalion	QM Company	Signal Company	Medical Co.	Airborne Antiaircraft Battalion	Ordnance Co	**Total**	Attached medical	Attached chaplain	**Total**
Major General	1												1			1
Brigadier General	1			1									2			2
Colonel	1			1	1	1							5			5
Lieutenant-colonel	11			4	4	3	1	1	1		1	1	30			30
Major	6	1	1	8	5	4	1			1	1		32	3		35
Major or Captain	1												1			1
Captain	11	1		27	23	17	7	2	1		8	2	116			116
Captain or 1st Lieutenant										16			16	32	7	5
First Lieutenant	5	3	1	40	62	28	9	2	1	4	8	2	193			193
Second Lieutenant	1	1		13	36	14	6			1	9	2	97			97
TOTAL COMMISSIONED	38	5	2	94	131	67	24	5	4	21	27	7	492	35	7	534
Warrant officer	6			8	5	3	2		1		1	1	30			30
Master Sergeant	9			6	5	4	1	2	2		1	1	35			35
First Sergeant		1		12	14	10	4	1	1	1	6	1	61			61
Technical Sergeant	4			18	6	25	4		3		4	3	92	3		95
Staff Sergeant	5	6	1	62	57	93	16	4	6	9	14	8	374	12		386
Sergeant	10	3	5	64	144	111	23	1		9	22	2	505	3		508
Corporal		3	3	165	154	33	27	7	5	8	66	1	505	11		516
Technician Grade 3	7			4				1	4			2	18			18
Technician Grade 4	27	7	2	80	76	34	17	3	11	8	22	11	332	17		349
Technician Grade 5	15	10	2	98	135	48	58	8	24	19	52	15	532	47		579
Private First Class		19	10	380	605	800	109	26	15	62	126	10	2962	75		3037
Private		26	13	476	622	380	142	33	24	79	163	15	2353	95		2448
TOTAL	77	75	36	1365	1818	1538	401	86	95	195	476	69	7769	263		8032
TOTAL	121	80	38	1467	1954	1608	427	91	100	216	504	77	8291	298	7	8596

ARMAMENT

	Division HQ	Div HQ Co.	MP Platoon	Division Artillery	Parachute Infantry Regiment [1]	2 Glider Infantry Regiment [2]	Engineer Battalion	QM Company	Signal Company	Medical Co.	Airborne Antiaircraft Battalion	Ordnance Co	**Total**	Attached medical	Attached chaplain	**Total**
Airplane, liaison				8									8			8
Parachutes				431	1749		139						2319	82	2	2403
Compressor, air, trailer							2						2			2
Tractor, crawler type, DBHP							4						4			4
Trailer, dump, 1/2 ton							10						10			10
Carbine, cal.30	93	79	33	1420	717	766	170	82	99		502	76	4803			4803
Cart, hand, M3A4					27	72	20				42		233			233
Cart, hand, M6A1											20		20			20
Gun, 57-mm anti-tank				4		8					24		44			44
Gun, machine, heavy, cal.30						8							16			16
Gun, machine, light, cal.30			2		132	12	21						179			179
Gun, machine, cal.50		3		56	4	3		4			36		111			111
Gun, submachine, cal.45			4		54	36	18		4				148			148
Howitzer, 75-mm, pack				36									36			36
Launcher, rocket, AT		101		177	73	73	25	5	4			5	445			445
Mortar, 60-mm					27	24							75			75
Mortar, 81-mm					12	12							36			36
Motorcycle, solo		2											2			2
Pistol, cal.45	18	1	1	48	10	8	2	1	1		2	1	101			101
Rifle, cal.30, M1					1227	792	255						3066			3066
Rifle, automatic, cal.30 (BAR)						42		8					92			92
Scooter, motor		4		46	52	29	20	4		4	15	2	205			205
Servicycle									9				9			9
Trailer, 1/4-ton		1	4	35	10	12	8	30	4	20	44	15	195	13	7	215
Trailer, 1-ton, cargo		13	1	27	16	16	4				2	5	87			87
Truck, 1/4-ton		9	4	97	15	20	19	30	4	23	44	15	300	16	7	325
Truck, 3/4-ton, ambulance										2			2			2
Truck, 3/4-ton, weapons		5		8	1	1					2		18			18
Truck, 2-1/2-ton		10		27	16	10	4				2	6	95			95
Flamethrower							3						3			3

The total strength of the Airborne Division on 6 June 1944, taking into account the changes made before this date was 11,432 officers, warrant officers and enlisted men.
Notes.
1. 6 June: 3 regiments
2. 6 June: One 3-battalion regiment

---

seemed secondary compared with what each Allied soldier was waiting for: a landing on the Northwest coast of Europe.

Indeed, in November 1943, the 82nd A/B div. (except for the 504th PIR which joined them only in May 1944 and so did not take part in Overlord) was shipped to Northern Ireland, then to England where it took part in countless manoeuvres with its sister unit, the 101st A/B div. 'Screaming Eagles'. The 101st had been formed in the USA with a cadre from the 82nd; it had come over to England in September 1943.

From their creation in 1942 until 1944, the airborne divisions' organization was modified many times mainly as a result of combat experience and the availability of air transport. In 1942, a typical division consisted of a total of 8, 505 men, with one regiment of parachute infantry and two of glider-borne infantry. In 1943, a new organizational plan considerably increased its strength which rose to 12,979 men with two parachute regiments and one of glider infantry. Finally at the beginning of 1944, this was brought back down to 7,500, by reducing the support component. There were three parachute infantry regiments with only a single Glider infantry two-battalion regiment.

Abbreviations used by the US Army and the US Army Air Forces

1LT	First Lieutenant	CP	Command post	Maint	Maintenance	SCR	Set, complete, radio
2LT	Second Lieutenant	CPL	Corporal	MAJ	Major	S	Submachine gun
AA	Antiaircraft	CPT	Captain	Mech	Mechanic	S-1 (2,3,4)	Staff sections
AAA	Antiaircraft Artillery	DC	Dental corps	Med	Medical	Sct	Scout
Abn	Airborne	Demo	Demolitions	Met	Meteorological	Sect	Section
Acrft	Aircraft	Det	Detachment	MG	Major General	SGT	Sergeant
ADC	Aide-de-camp	Div	Division	MMG	Cal.30 machinegun, medium	Sig.	Signal
Adj	Adjudant	DS	Direct support			SigC	Signal corps
Admin	Administrative	DZ	Drop Zone	MO	Medical Officer	Slt	Searchlight
AG	Adjudant General			Mort	Mortar	Smbl	Semi mobile
AGF	Army Ground Forces	EM	Enlisted man	Mot	Motor	SNL	Standard nomenclature listing
Agt	Agent	Engr	Engineer	MP	Military police		
ALO	Air liaison officer	Equip	Equipment	MSG	Master sergeant	SGM	Sergeant major
Amb	Ambulance	FA	Field artillery	Msg Ctr	Message center	SMG	Submachine gun
Ammo	Ammunition	FAC	Forward air controller	Msgr	Messenger	SP	Self propelled
Amph	Amphibious	FDC	Fire direction center	Mtcl	Motorcycle	Sqd	Squad
Aobsr	Air observer	FM	Field manual	Mtd	Mounted	Sqdn	Squadron
AR	Automatic rifle	FO	Forward observer	Mtr	Motor	SSG	Staff sergeant
A/car	Armored car	FSG	First sergeant	Mun	Munitions	Sur	Surgeon
Armd	Armored	Fwd	Forward	NCO	Non-commissioned officer	Swbd	Switchboard
Arty	Artillery	G-1 (2,3,4)	General staff section	O	Observer		
AT	Antitank	GIR	Glider Infantry Regiment	Obsv	Observation	TCG	Troop Carrier Group
Autmv	Automotive	GL	Grenade launcher	OP	Observation post	TCS	Troop Carrier Squadron
Auto	Automatic		C: Carbine	Ops	Operations	TCW	Troop Carrier Wing
AW	Automatic weapons		R: Rifle	Opr	Operator	T/BA	Table of basic allowances
BC	Battery commander	Gnr	Gunner	Ord	Ordnance	T/E	Table of equipment
BG	Brigadier General	H & S	Headquarters & Service	P & A	Pioneer & ammunition	T/O & E	Table of organization & equipment
Bde	Brigade	HH	Headquarters & headquarters (Co.)	P	Pistol, Cal.45		
Bn	Battalion			PFC	Private first class	T/O	Table of organization
Btry	Battery	HHS	HQ, HQ & service	Pion	Pioneer	Tech 3	Technician 3rd grade (4, 5)
C	Carbine	HMG	Cal.50 machinegun	PIR	Parachute Infantry Regiment	Tech	Technical
C & R	Command & recon.	How	Howitzer	Plat	Platoon	Tg	Telegraph
Cal	Caliber	Hq (HQ)	Headquarters	POL	Petroleum, oil & lubricants	Tk	Tank
Cav	Cavalry	H/trk	Half track	Prcht	Parachute	Tlr	Trailer
CC	Combat command	Hvy	Heavy	Ptbl	Portable	Topo	Topography, topographic
CF	Counter fire	I & R	Intelligence & Recon	PVT	Private	Tp opr	Telephone operator
Cfr	Chauffeur	Inf	Infantry	QM	Quartermaster	Tp	Telephone
CG	Commanding General	Inst	Instrument			Trac	Tractor
Ch	Chief	Intel	Intelligence	R	Rifle	Trk	Truck
CM	Counter mortar	Lchr	Launcher	R03	Rifle M1903	Trp	Troop
CO	Commanding Officer	Ldr	Leader	Rad	Radio	TSG	Technical sergeant
Co	Company	LMG	Cal.30 machine gun, light	Rcl	Recoilless	TT	Teletype
CofS	Chief of staff	Ln O	Liaison officer	Rcn	Reconnaissance		
COL	Colonel	Lt	Light	Recon	Reconnaissance	Veh	Vehicle
COE	Cab over engine	LTC	Lieutenant colonel	Rgt	Regiment	Wkr	Wrecker
Com	Communications	LZ	Landing zone	Rkt	Rocket	WO	Warrant officer
Cmd	Command			RO	Reconnaissance officer	Wpn	Weapon
Cmdr	Commander	MAC	Medical administrative corps			XO	Executive Officer

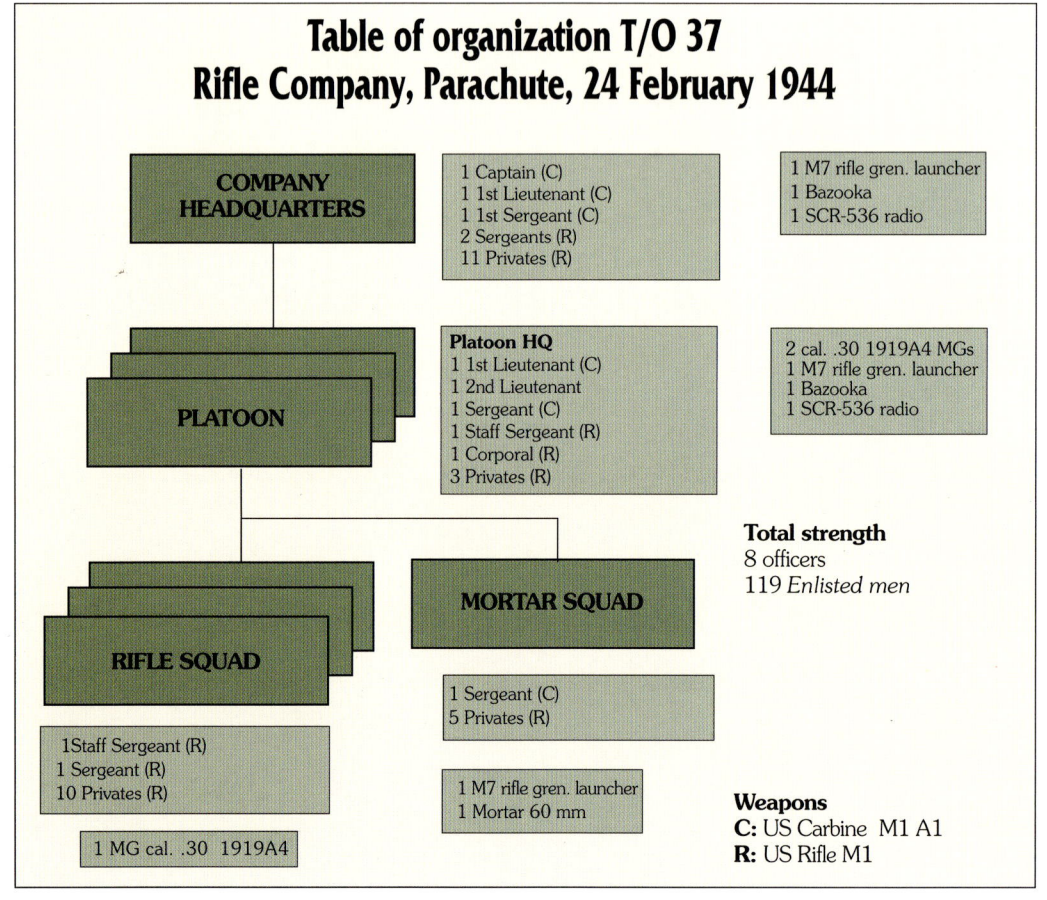

Table of organization T/O 37
Rifle Company, Parachute, 24 February 1944

COMPANY HEADQUARTERS
- 1 Captain (C)
- 1 1st Lieutenant (C)
- 1 1st Sergeant (C)
- 2 Sergeants (R)
- 11 Privates (R)
- 1 M7 rifle gren. launcher
- 1 Bazooka
- 1 SCR-536 radio

PLATOON
Platoon HQ
- 1 1st Lieutenant (C)
- 1 2nd Lieutenant
- 1 Sergeant (C)
- 1 Staff Sergeant (R)
- 1 Corporal (R)
- 3 Privates (R)
- 2 cal. .30 1919A4 MGs
- 1 M7 rifle gren. launcher
- 1 Bazooka
- 1 SCR-536 radio

RIFLE SQUAD
- 1 Staff Sergeant (R)
- 1 Sergeant (R)
- 10 Privates (R)
- 1 MG cal. .30 1919A4

MORTAR SQUAD
- 1 Sergeant (C)
- 5 Privates (R)
- 1 M7 rifle gren. launcher
- 1 Mortar 60 mm

Total strength
8 officers
119 Enlisted men

Weapons
C: US Carbine M1 A1
R: US Rifle M1

Opposite, top.
'The Americans have arrived!' Ever since dawn on the 6th, the truth was bursting out, causing great joy among the Normans, and the welcome given to these paratroopers from the 101st Airborne taking a breather in the hamlet of Ecoqueneauville is heartfelt. Note the wide strips of felt padding under the suspenders of the second man from the right.
(National Archives)

Opposite, bottom
This newly-found freedom was celebrated heartily everywhere: wines bottles were dug out from under wood piles and cider barrels were broached. And the generous helpings of apple brandy (Calvados) went down especially well with the paratroopers. There were however cases where the liberators were wary and got their hosts to take a drink first: hadn't some of them been told that the majority of Frenchmen had been evacuated and that those who were allowed to remain in their homes were the collaborator friends of the Germans?
(National Archives)

"LA FAYETTE, we have returned!"

The Normans who lived in the Cotentin peninsula were waiting for their liberators, expecting them to charge out of the midday sun, flags unfurled and trumpets blaring…

They got their money's worth: freedom fell to earth from a dark night sky, but their liberators came to them like thieves, cropping up behind hedges, stealthily tip-toeing on their Goodyear rubber-soled jump boots.

Twenty-seven years to the day after the first time they came to France, on 13 June 1917, the Americans were back, in strength this time and intending to get a foothold on the Old Continent, which was almost entirely under the yoke of Nazi Germany.

The vanguard of this powerful army built up in less than three years, consisted of airborne divisions which had to open up the way in Normandy for the troops coming from the sea and whose gigantic armada was lashing about on the gray seas of the Channel on this, the eve of Liberation.

But the first contacts with the locals were sometimes brutal, often the black muzzle of a rifle prodded into the stomach.

Near Sainte-Mère-Eglise, liberation turned to tragedy when a young Frenchman was shot dead in front of his family by a burst of sub-machine gun fire from paratroopers who had received orders to 'kill everything.'

But horror also came from the enemy. In a modest cottage, in the hamlet of 'La Barquette', three children were doused with petrol and turned into living torches by a German soldier who went mad because the Third Reich was suffering defeat after defeat…

It is not possible to give an accurate figure for civilian casualties on 6 June. However, if the Calvados Department holds the record for death and destruction, the Manche Department also paid a heavy tribute for freedom. At the end of the Battle of Normandy there were more than 3,500 killed and 280,000 homeless out of a population of 480,000. 60,000 dwellings were utterly destroyed and towns like Périers, Saint-Lô, Montebourg and Valognes were in ruins.

Jean Bouchery

THE 82nd AIRBORNE DIVISION CHAIN OF COMMAND

(Order of battle on 6 June 1944)

Division commander
Major Gen. Matthew B. Ridgway
Executives
— Brigadier General James Maurice Gavin
— Brigadier General George P. Howell
Chief of staff
— Colonel Ralph Eaton, *wounded on June 6, then*
— Colonel Edson R. Raff, *8-15 June, then*
— Lieutenant-colonel R. Wienecke
G-1. *(Personnel)*
— Lieutenant-colonel Frederick Schellhammer
G-2. *(Intelligence)*
— Lieutenant-colonel Jack Whitfield
G-3. *(Operations)*
— Colonel Walter Winton
G-4. *(Supply)*
— Lieutenant-colonel Bennie A. Zinn, *wounded on June 7, then*
— Lt.-Col. Frank W. Moorman

● **505th Parachute Infantry Regiment**
Colonel William E. Ekman
— I/505
Major Frederick A. Kellam
— II/505
Lieutenant-colonel Benjamin H. Vandervoort
— III/505
Lieutenant-colonel Edward C. Krause, *wounded on June 6, then* Major Hagan

● **507th Parachute Infantry Regiment**
Colonel George Millett, *captured on June 8, then*
Lieutenant-colonel Maloney, *then* Colonel Edson D. Raff *on June 15*.
— I/507: Lieutenant colonel Edwin Ostberg
— II/507: Lieutenant-colonel Charles Timmes
— III/507: Lieutenant colonel Arthur Maloney

● **508th Parachute Infantry Regiment**
Colonel Roy E. Linquist
— I/508
Major Shields Warren
— II/508
Lieutenant-colonel Thomas J. B. Shanley
— III/508
Lieutenant-Colonel Louis G. Mendez

● **Pathfinder group**
1st Lieutenant Charles Ames

● **325th Glider Infantry Regiment**
Colonel Harry L. Lewis
— I/325
Lieutenant-colonel Major T. Sanford
— II/325
Lieutenant-colonel J.H. Swenson
— III/401
Lt. Col. C. Carrel, *replaced on June 9 by* Major A. Gardner

● **456th Para. Field Artillery Bn.**
Lt. Col. W. d'Alessio
● **319th Glider Field Artillery Bn.**
Lt. Col. J. Todd
● **320 Glider Field Artillery Bn.**
Lt. Col. Paul E. Wright
● **80th Airborne AAA Bn.**
Lt. Col. R. Singleton
● **307th Airborne Engineer Bn.**
Lt. Col. Robert Palmer

● **Other units**
— 782d Ordnance Co.
— 82d Signal Co.
— 407th Quartermaster Co.
— 307th Medical Co.
— 82d Parachute maintenance Co.
— 82d Military police platoon

CAMPAIGNS
Sicily: 9 July 1943
Italy, Naples: 13 September 1943
Normandy: 6 juin 1944
Bulge: 18 December 1944
Germany: 2 April 1945.
The division was inactivated in the US on 27 March 1946.

1944 Conventional Map Reading signs

☐	Unit
⊠	Infantry (glider: GLI, parachute: ⌒)
⊘	Cavalry (recon.)
E	Engineers
●	Artillery
S	Signals
△	Artillery (incl. Antiaircraft & Antitank)
♛	Ordnance
⚲	Quartermaster
MP	Military Police
✚	Medical
⬭	Tank, Armored
TD	Tank Destroyer
Band	Band

Major-General Matthew Bunker Ridgway.
This Virginian was a graduate of West Point and had been in command of the 82nd Airborne since 1942. The first American airborne division fought in Sicily under his command. Two months after Operation 'Neptune,' Ridgway took command of the XVIII Airborne Corps.

BG James M. Gavin, second in command of the 82nd A/B div., had enlisted as a private in 1924 at the age of seventeen and graduated from West Point in 1929. He was thought to be one of the best American generals of the war. He took command of the division in August 1944. *(National Archives)*

Brigadier General Maxwell Taylor was appointed to command the 101st A/B division on 14 March 1944 after having served in the 82nd, among other things. He was a courageous and dynamic general and Normandy was his first operational jump.
(National Archives)

THE 101st AIRBORNE DIVISION CHAIN OF COMMAND
(Order of battle on 6 June 1944)

Division commander
— Major General Maxwell D. Taylor
Executive
— Brigadier General Don F. Pratt, *killed on June 6,* then
— Brigadier General Anthony McAuliffe (div. artillery cmder)
Chief of Staff
— Col. G. Higgins, *replaces* Don Pratt on June 6
G-1. (Personnel)
— Colonel Ned D. Moore
G-2. (Intelligence)
— Colonel Arthur M. Sommerfield
G-3. (Operations)
— Colonel Millener
G4. (Supply)
— Colonel Carl W. Kohls

● **501st Parachute Infantry Regiment**
Colonel Howard Johnson
— **I/501**
Lieutenant-colonel Robert Caroll, *died on June 6*
— **II/501**
Lieutenant-colonel Robert Ballard
— **III/501**
Lieutenant-colonel Julian Ewell

● **502d Parachute Infantry Regiment**
Colonel George Moseley, *wounded on June 6,* then
Lieutenant-colonel John Michaelis
— **I/502**
Lieutenant-colonel Patrick Cassidy
— **II/502**
Lieutenant colonel Steve Chappuis, *wounded on June 6*
— **III/502**
Lieutenant-colonel Robert Cole

● **506th Parachute Infantry Regiment**
Colonel Robert Sink
— **I/506**
Lieutenant-colonel Turner
— **II/506**
Lieutenant-colonel Robert Strayer
— **III/506**
Lieutenant-colonel Robert Wolverton, *killed on June 6*

● **327th Glider Infantry Regiment**
Colonel George S. Wear, *then* Colonel J.H. Harper
— **I/327**
Lieutenant-colonel Hartford F. Sales
— **II/327**
Lieutenant-colonel Thomas J. Rouzie
— **I/401**
Lieutenant-colonel Ray C. Allen

● **Pathfinder group (502nd)**
Captain Frank Lillyman

● **377th Parachute Field Artillery Bn.**
Lieutenant-colonel B. Weisberg
● **321st Glider Field Artillery Bn.**
Lieutenant-colonel Edward L. Carmichael
● **907th Glider Field Artillery Bn.**
Lieutenant-colonel Clarence F. Nelson
● **81st Airborne Anti-Aircraft/Anti Tank Bn.**
Lieutenant-colonel X. B. Cox
● **326th Airborne Engineer Bn.**
Colonel F. A. Stanlley

● **Other units:**
— 801st Ordnance Co.
— 101st Signal Co.
— 426th Quartermaster Co.
— 101st Parachute Maintenance Co
— 101st Military Police Platoon.

CAMPAIGNS
— **Normandy:** 6 June 1944 to 13 July 1944
— **Holland** (Nijmegen)**:** from 17 September 1944
— **Bulge:** 18 December 1944
— **Germany:** April 1944.
The division was inactivated in France on 30 November 1945.

Opposite.
Brigadier-General Donald F. Pratt (center).
The Second-in-command of the 101st Airborne Division did not fight in France: his glider crashed into a tree on landing and he was killed instantly.
(National Archives)

US Army Field Units

XXXX — Army	XXX — Army corps	XX — Division
III — Regiment	II — Battalion	I — Company, Troop
••• — Platoon	•• — Section	• — Squad
X — Brigade (Combat Command)		Headquarters or Small Unit

13

THE AMERICAN AIRBORNE

- Divisional HQ
- HQ Co
- Chaplain
- Civil Affairs
- Band
- 82d Recon Platoon
- M P — 82d Military Police Platoon
- CIC — 82d Counter Intelligence Detachment

- Pathfinder Group
- 505 PIR
- 507 PIR
- 508 PIR

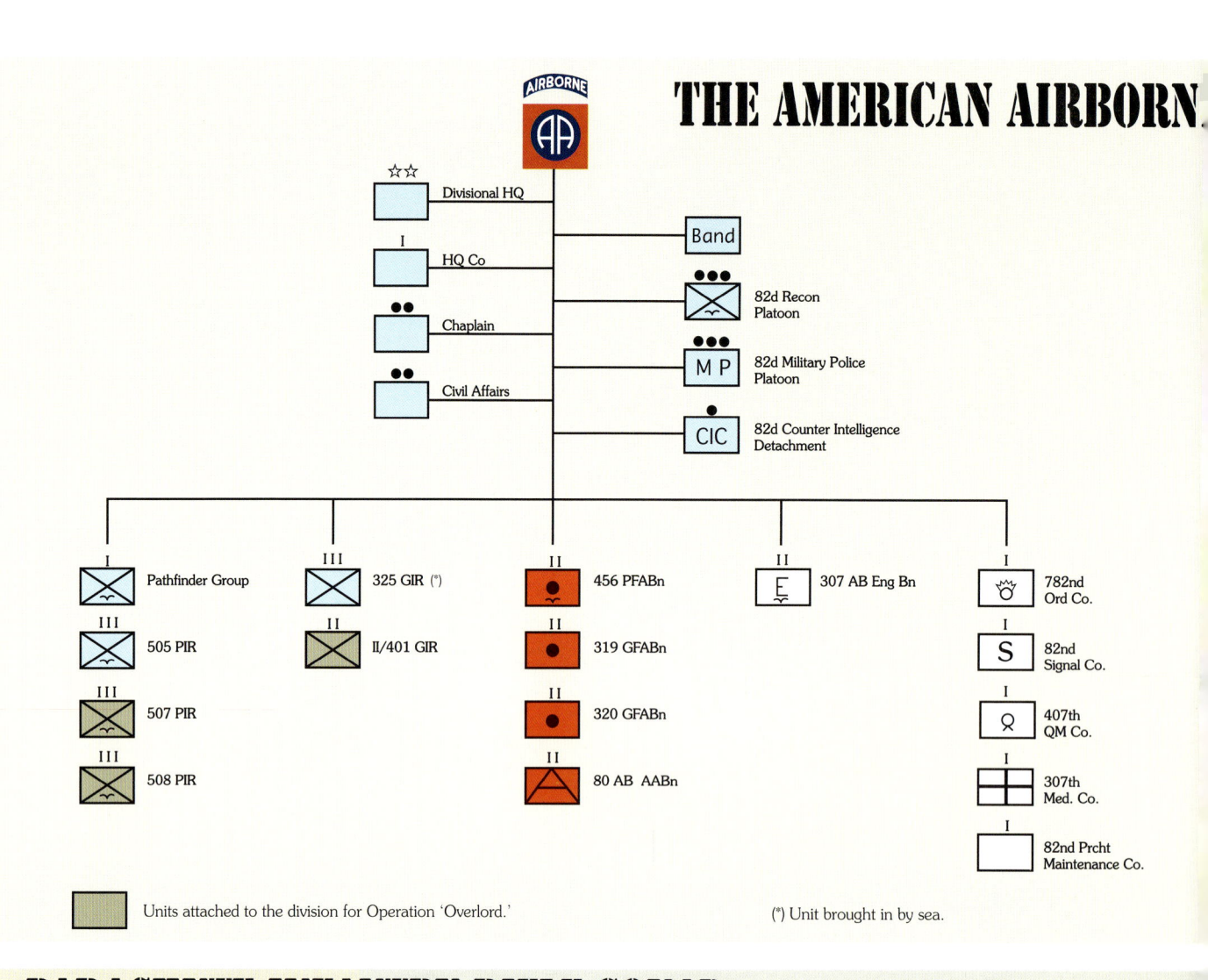

- 325 GIR (*)
- II/401 GIR

- 456 PFABn
- 319 GFABn
- 320 GFABn
- 80 AB AABn

- 307 AB Eng Bn

- 782nd Ord Co.
- 82nd Signal Co.
- 407th QM Co.
- 307th Med. Co.
- 82nd Prcht Maintenance Co.

Units attached to the division for Operation 'Overlord.'

(*) Unit brought in by sea.

PARACHUTE INFANTRY RIFLE SQUAD (T/O 24 February 1944)

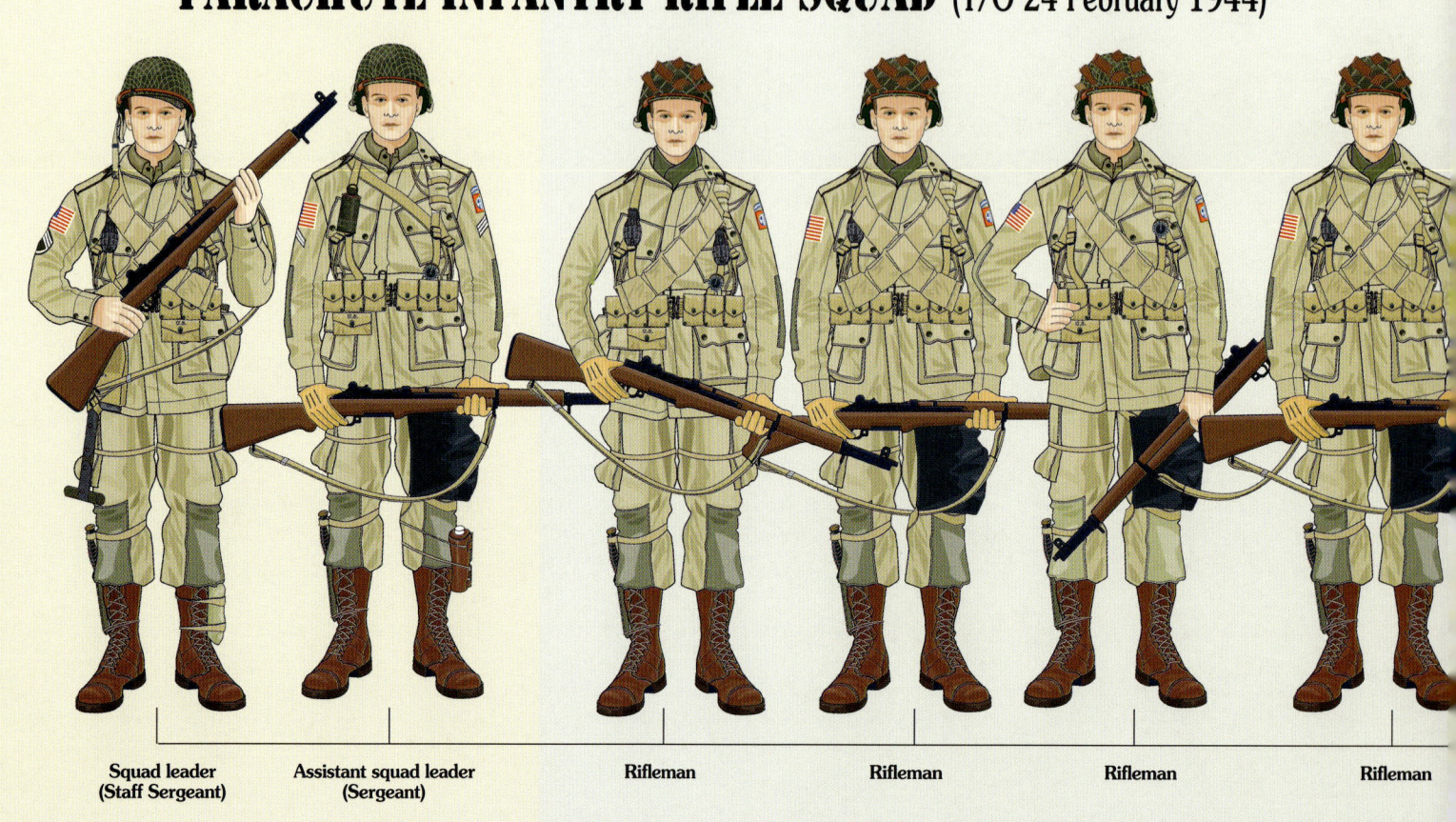

Squad leader (Staff Sergeant) | Assistant squad leader (Sergeant) | Rifleman | Rifleman | Rifleman | Rifleman

DIVISIONS, JUNE 6 1944

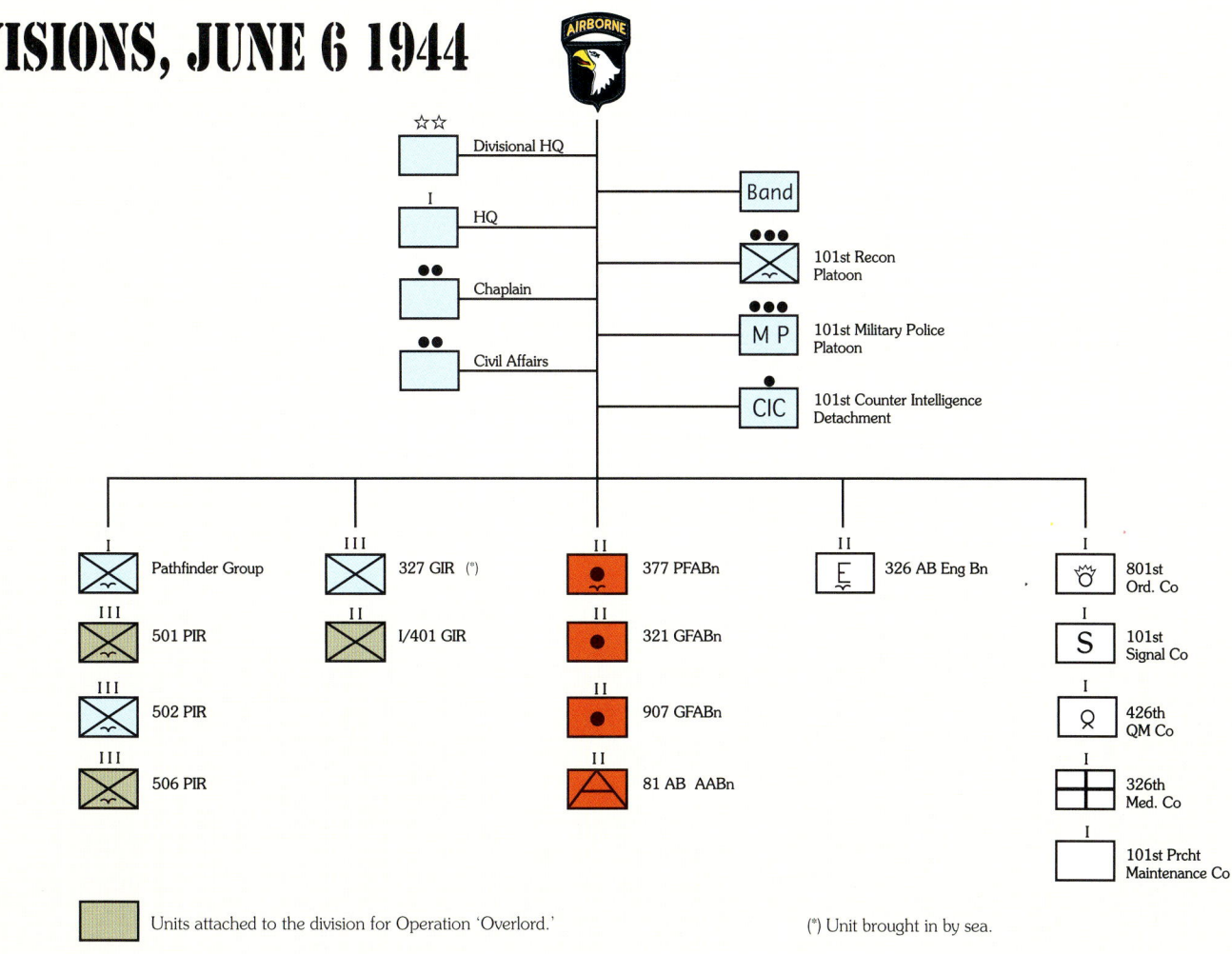

Note.
All squad members armed with M1 rifle, except light machine gunner who has a carbine. The Feb. 1944 T/O canceled the pistol issue to all squad members but in June 1944, some infantrymen still had one and it can be seen on several of the figures below.

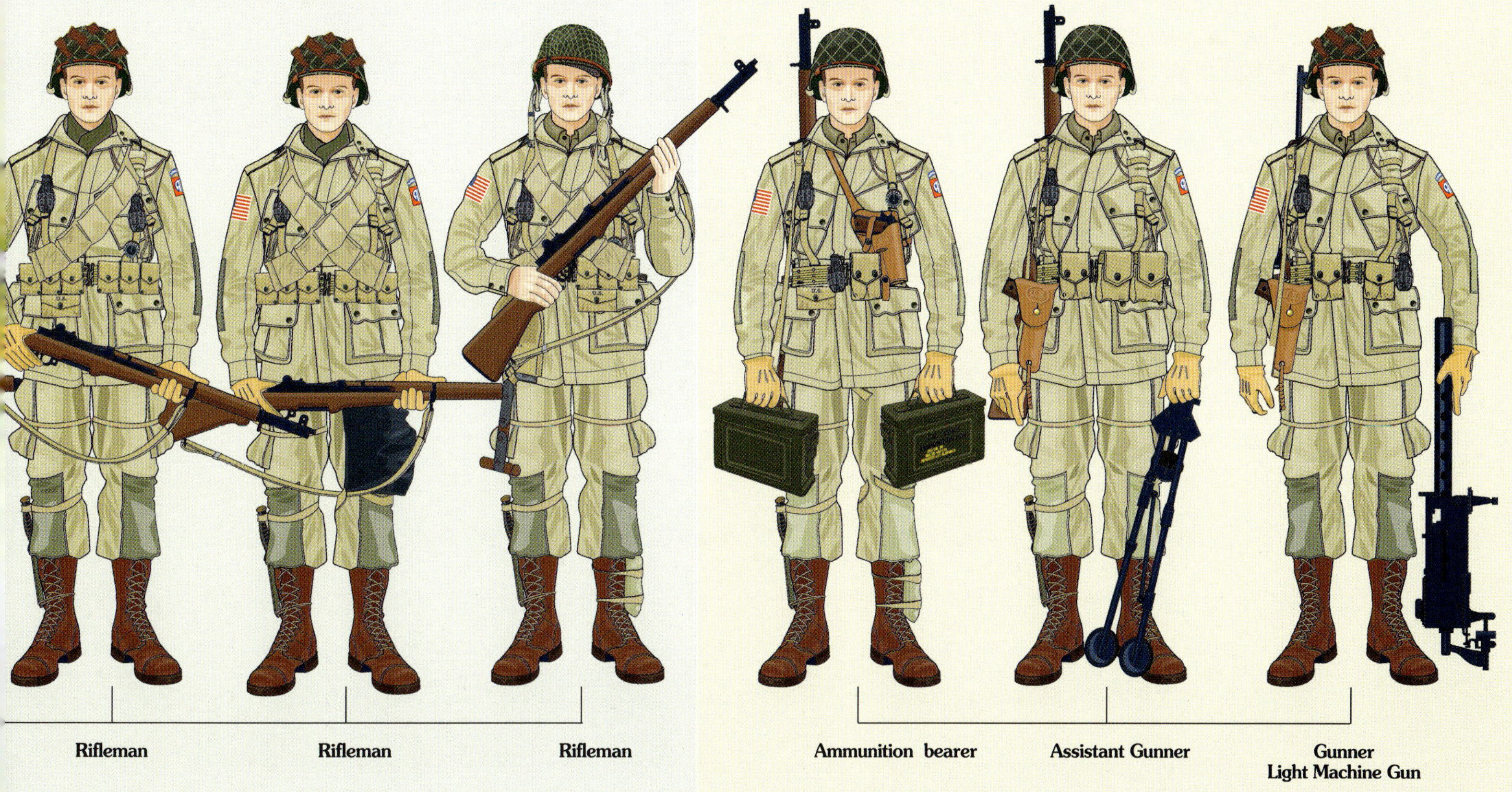

| Rifleman | Rifleman | Rifleman | Ammunition bearer | Assistant Gunner | Gunner Light Machine Gun |

(Computer graphics by Andre Jouineau, © 2004 Histoire & Collections

CHAPTER 2: THE 9TH AIR FORCE'S IX TROOP CARRIER COMMAND

9th Air Force shoulder sleeve insignia and non-regulation 'Airborne' tab for troop carrier units

Non-regulation Troop Carrier Command insignia

Activated in England in October 1943, the IX Troop Carrier Command was attached to the 9th Air Force. Its mission was to air lift the airborne divisions and ensure they were supplied during the forthcoming operations.

It was based at Grantham after 1 December 1943 and was commanded by General Paul L. Williams.

In order to carry out its missions, the IX Troop Carrier Command had extensive means required given the size and scale of the task.

The planes used for the Normandy operation were the following: the twin-engined Douglas C-47 (Skytrooper), the American CG-4A Waco glider and the British Horsa glider.

The Douglas C-47

Derived from the civilian DC-3 airliner which made its maiden flight in 1935, it was a modern plane, unrivaled at the time. The C-47 was adopted and ordered in very large numbers by the US Army Air Forces from the end of 1941. In ten years of production, more than 13,000 were made. In 1944 only, 4,878 C-47s came off the assembly lines.

True beasts of burden, they were very reliable and robust, and continued their military and civilian careers worldwide a long time after the war.

The crew consisted of four men:
- pilot
- co-pilot
- navigator
- Jump (load) master.

The C-47 could carry 18 paratroopers in full combat dress. Containers could be attached to the belly of the aircraft. The C-47s were also used as glider tugs.

The CG-4A Waco Glider

Designed by the Waco aircraft Company at the request of the US Army Air Forces, the CG-4A was ordered in May 1942 and more than 14,000 were produced by 16 different companies from June 1942 to 1945.

The wings and the tail were built of wood, the fuselage being made of a tubular structure covered with fabric.

The CG-4A could carry 15 fully-equipped soldiers, a 75-mm howitzer or a light bulldozer.

In order to unload men and equipment rapidly, the nose was hinged just aft the cockpit. A metal structure called a 'Griswold nose' was often mounted on the front of the machine to protect the crews from obstacles encountered when landing.

The glider landed on two wheels and three skids situated at the front of the plane.

During the operations in Normandy, the Wacos were used preferably for night operations as they were more easily handled and smaller than the British Horsa. Their tubular structure turned out to be very strong during hairy landings.

The British Airspeed Horsa glider

Designed by Airspeed Limited to answer the needs of the British Airborne troops, the Horsa was mass-produced from March 1942. Most of the glider was made of fabric covered plywood.

More than 3,800 Horsas of all versions were built between 1942 and 1945.

The Horsa could carry 26 fully-equipped men plus the two-man crew, or two jeeps or one jeep and a 75-mm howitzer, or a 57-mm anti-tank gun and a jeep.

Loading was done through a wide side door just aft the cockpit. After landing, the fuselage could be split in two for quick unloading.

The Horsa was used during the day preferably as its large size and weight gave it a high landing speed, obliging the pilots to look for larger and clearer landing zones than for the CG-4A. In the case of a very rough landing, the structure of the Horsa would often burst, producing slivers of wood which were very dangerous for the passengers.

Major-General Paul L. Williams commanding IX Troop Carrier Command. He very efficiently organised supplies and air transport for the airborne divisions during the various operations in North-West Europe.
(National Archives)

IX Troop Carrier Command

(CG: General Paul L. Williams, based at Grantham from 1 December 1943)

Troop Carrier WING	Troop Carrier GROUP	Troop Carrier SQUADRON	PLANE CODE	BASE	Commanding officer	ASSIGNMENTS
50th TCW Based at Exeter Brigadier General Julian Chappell	439th	91st 92nd 93rd 94th	L4 J8 3B D8	Upottery	Col. Charles H. Young	Dropped 1/506 and 2/506 of the 101 A/B; supply and reinforcement missions by glider.
	440th	95th 96th 97th 98th	9X 6Z W6 8Y	Exeter	Lt. Col X. Krebs	Dropped 3/506 of the 101 A/B in the Carentan area, then supply and reinforcement missions until 7 June.
	441st	99th 100th 301st 302nd	3J 8C Z4 2L	Merryfield	Col. Theodore G. Shaw	Dropped 1/501 and 2/501 of the 101 A/B; supply and reinforcement operations by glider.
	442nd	303rd 304th 305th 306th	J7 V4 4J 7H	Fulbeck	Col. Charles M. Smith	Dropped paratroopers of 1/507 of the 82nd Airborne over Ste-Mère-Eglise, then supply missions over the same sector.
52rd TCW Based at Cottesmore Brigadier General Harold L. Clark	61st	14th 15th 53rd 59th	3I Y9 3A X5	Barkston	Col. Willis W. Mitchell	Dropped men of 2/507 and 3/507 of the 82 A/B and equipment.
	313rd	29th 47th 48th 49th	Z7 N3 5X H2	Folkingham	Col. James J. Roberts	Dropped paratroopers of 1/508 and 2/508 of the 82 A/B over Picauville on 6 June, and brought in reinforcements during the 7th.
	314th	32nd 50th 61st 62nd	S2 2R Q9 E5	Saltby	Col. Clayton Stiles	Dropped men of 3/508 (82 A/B) and ammunition
	315th	34th 43rd 309th 310th	NM UA M6 4A	Stanhoe	Col. Hamish Mc Lalland	Dropped 1/501, 307th Engineers, and elements of the 82 A/B HQ.
	442nd	303rd 304th 305th 306th	J7 V4 4J 7H	Fulbeck	Col. Charles M. Smith	Dropped parachutists of 2/505, 3/505 and 456th PFABn of the 82 A/B over Sainte-Mère-Eglise on 6 June.
53rd TCW Based at Greenham Common Brigadier General Maurice M. Beach	434th	71st 72nd 73rd 74th	CJ CU CN ID	Alder Maston	Col. William B. Whitecare	Brought in gliders (missions 'Chicago' and 'Keokuk') and numerous other supply missions.
	435th	75th 76th 77th 78th	SH CW IB CM	Welford	Col. Frank J. Mc Nees	Dropped 3/501 of the 101 A/B during the morning of 6 June, glider tugs in the afternoon (mission 'Elmira').
	436th	79th 80th 81st 82nd	S6 7D U5 3D	Membury	Col. Adrian N. Williams	Dropped 1/502 and elements of 377th PFABn of the 82 A/B on 6 June; supply and reinforcement missions by glider (mission 'Elmira').
	437th	83rd 84th 85th 86th	T2 Z8 9O 5K	Ramsbury	Col. Cedric E. Hudgens	On the morning of the 6 June, brought in gliders (mission Elmira) and carried out supply missions for the 82 A/B.
	438th	87th 88th 89th 90th	3X M2 4U Q7	Greenham	Col. John M. Donaldson	Dropped 2/502, 3/502 and elements of the 377th PFABn, towing gliders (mission 'Elmira').
		X Troop Carrier Pathfinder Group (Provisional)		North Witham	Lt. Col. Crouch	Dropping pathfinder sticks from 82 and 101 AB on the DZ and LZ to mark out with beacons.

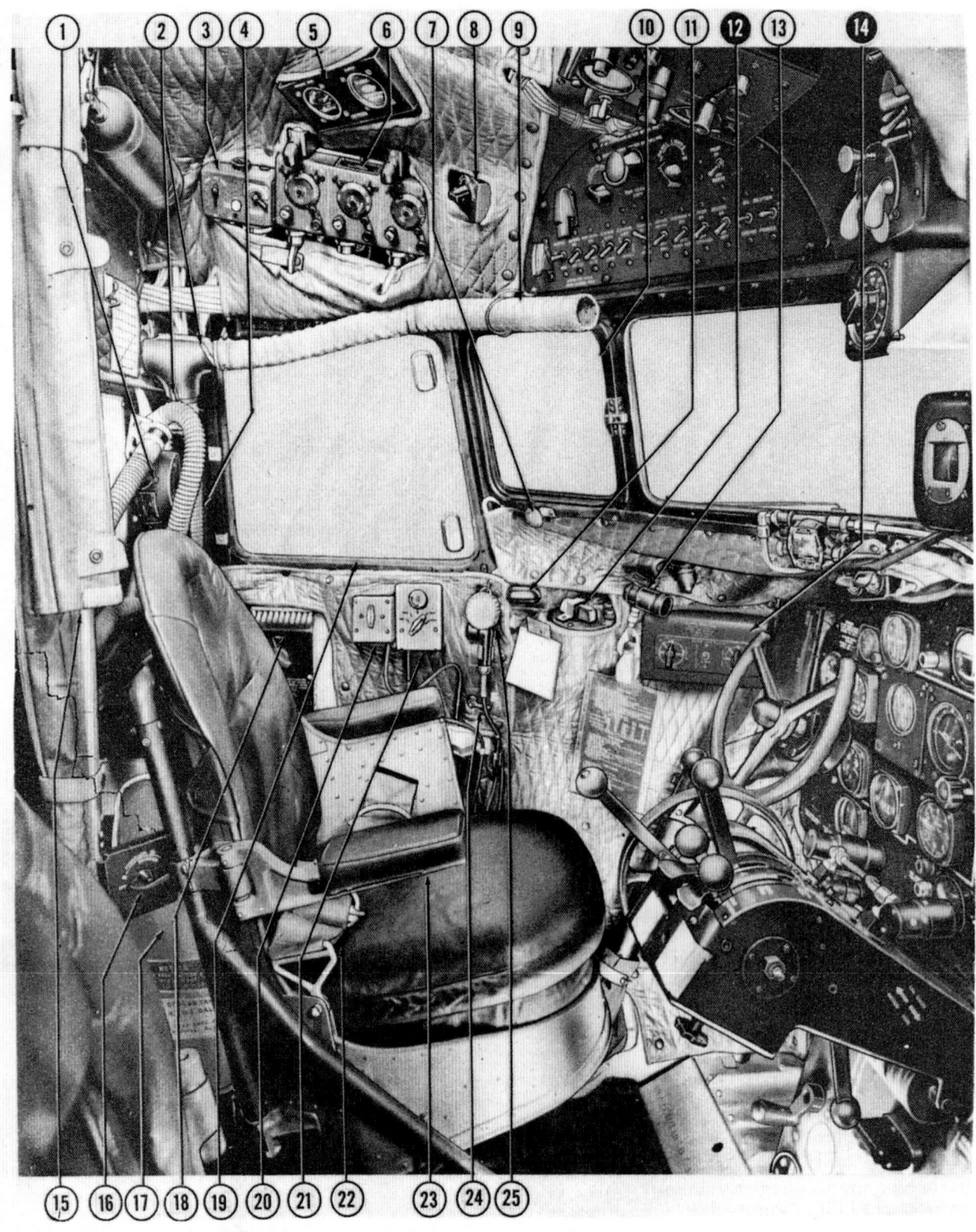

1. Oxygen Regulator and Hose
2. Windshield and Hand Warmer Butterfly Valves
3. Command Radio Transmitter Control Box
4. Flexible Hand Warmer and Spot Defroster
5. Oxygen Gage Panel
6. Command Radio Receiver Control Box
7. Windshield Friction Lock Knob
8. Radio Panel Lights (Late Airplanes)
9. Windshield Defroster Hose
10. Clear Vision Windshield Panel
11. Shielded Lamp
12. Blowers Control (Inoperative)
13. Fluorescent Lamp
14. Carburetor Air Induction Controls (Early Airplanes)
15. Pilot's Curtain
16. Propeller Anti-Icer Rheostat Control and Switch
17. Propeller De-Icer Supply Tank
18. Suit Heat Rheostat
19. Sliding Side Panel
20. Radio Filter Box
21. Interphone Junction Box
22. Safety Belt
23. Pilot's Seat
24. Windshield Alcohol De-Icer V Control
25. Microphone

Figure 8—Pilots' Compartment, Left Side

The C-47 cockpit layout on the pilot's side, as described in the Flight Operating Instructions Handbook, used for training pilots.

IX TROOP CARRIER UNITS INSIGNIA

61st Troop Carrier Group

315th Troop Carrier Group

14th Troop Carrier Squadron   53rd Troop Carrier Squadron   43rd Troop Carrier Squadron

WING 52

313rd Troop Carrier Group

29th Troop Carrier Squadron   47th Troop Carrier Squadron   49th Troop Carrier Squadron

435th Troop Carrier Group

75th Troop Carrier Squadron   76th Troop Carrier Squadron   77th Troop Carrier Squadron   78th Troop Carrier Squadron

437th Troop Carrier Group

438th Troop Carrier Group

WING 53

85th Troop Carrier Squadron   87th Troop Carrier Squadron

AIRCRAFT AND GLIDERS USED DURING AMERICAN AIRBORNE OPERATIONS ON 6 JUNE 1944

The British Horsa Glider

Horsa glider belonging to the 78th TCS of the 435th TCG, 53rd Wing based at Welford. Mission 'Elmira.' It took off at 20.40 hrs to reach Landing Zone W (Les Forges) at 23.05 hrs. It was piloted by First Lieutenant Howard Parks. The plane's nickname was 'Maja'.

Wingspan: 88 ft 6 in
Length: 67 ft 4 in
Weight, empty: 8,580 lbs
Normal loaded: 15,450 lbs
Max. towing speed: 156 mph
Landing Speed: 75 mph.

C-47 pilot's seat found in a Norman farm and recovered from the wreck of one of the machines shot down on 6 June 1944.
(Musée de la Seconde Guerre mondiale, Ambleteuse, Pas-de-Calais)

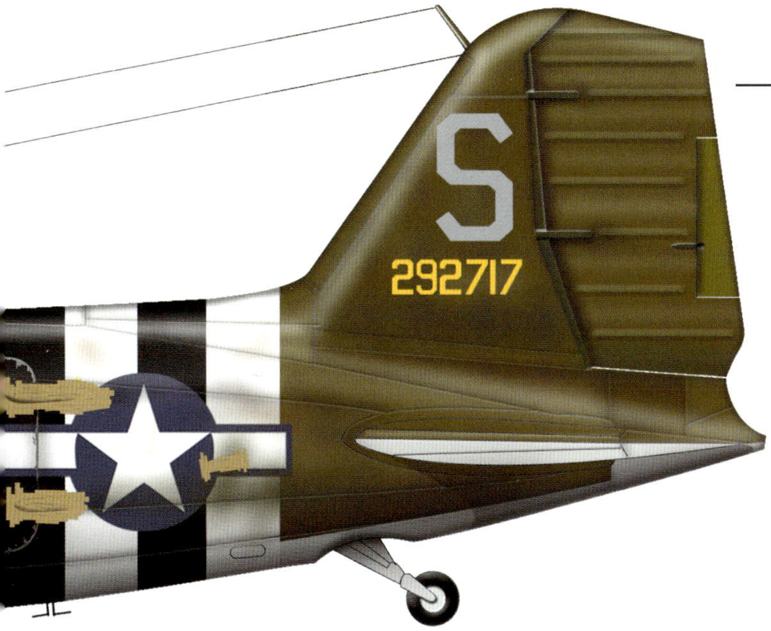

Douglas C-47

C-47 belonging to the HQ Squadron of the 440th Troop Carrier Group based at Exeter.
It was flown by Lieutenant-Colonel Krebs, 440th commanding officer. On board among others was Lieutenant-Colonel Wolverton, commanding 3/606th PIR (101st A/B).
Take off time 23.50, on target (DZ 'D,' Angoville-au-Plain) at 01.45.
As lead-ship, it was equipped with the SCR-717 radar whose radome is visible under the fuselage, and a 'Rebecca' receiver (the antenna can be seen near the cockpit).

The American CG-4A Waco Glider

CG-4A Waco glider of the 434th TCG (53rd Wing) based at Aldermaston, mission 'Chicago.' Take-off time 01.19 hrs, on target (LZ E, Hiesville) at 03.54 hrs. This glider carried General Don Pratt, the 101st Div. second in command, who died when it crashed on landing. The pilot, Lieutenant-colonel Murphy, broke both legs. The 'Fighting Falcon' had been funded by high school students from Greenville (Michigan).

Wingspan: 56 ft 2 in.
Length: 32 ft 5 in.
Weight, empty: 3700 lbs
Normal loaded: 7480 lbs.

(Computer graphics by Nicolas Gohin, © Histoire & Collections 2004)

C-47 PILOTS

C-47 pilot of the IX Troop Carrier Command. England, 5 June 1944

This pilot is wearing the officer's service cap. Its fashionable 'soft' shape had been obtained by removing the crown stiffener, thence the nickname 'Fifty Mission Crush'. The generic insignia of the Troop Carrier Command is sewn on the leather A-2 Flying Jacket sleeve. The officer's nameplate can be seen on the chest. An RAF survival whistle has been attached to the collar hook. The M-1911 A1 pistol in its leather holster is suspended from the M-1936 belt, which also supports an M-1923 magazine pocket. Issue serge trousers, leggings and service shoes make up the rest of the equipment.
(Reconstruction, photograph by Militaria Magazine)

Above.
Pilot's identity card, wristwatch with 'hack' synchronization feature, identity bracelet, pilot wings and matchbook from Stout Field, an I Troop Carrier Command stateside airbase.

AIRCREW

England, 5 June 1944 in the afternoon. An Airforce NCO poses for the photographer before leaving for Normandy.

The dress and equipment of this aircrew member worn here illustrate one of the many possibilities seen on period photographs.

- B-10 Flying jacket.
- Issue serge trousers.
- Leggings.
- Service shoes with toe cap.
- Garrison cap with USAAF (orange and ultramarine blue) piping and enamel Troop Carrier Command distinctive insignia.
- RAF pattern 1941 'Mae West' Life-belt.
- Leather gloves.
- HS-33 radio earphones.
- M3 Flak Helmet.
- AN-6530 Goggles.
- M3 Chest (Pistol) holster modified so that it can be worn on the waist.
- M-1911 A1 Automatic Pistol.
- Belt, Pistol M-1936.
- M-1923 magazine pocket.

The issue wool trousers and canvas leggings were worn for practical reasons in case crew members were shot down over Normandy, so they could join the troops on the ground before being sent back to England.

(Reconstruction)

THE GLIDER PILOTS

When the United States Army decided to use gliders for airborne assaults, pilots had to be found and trained urgently. 6,000 candidates from very diverse backgrounds were selected: civilian pilots, pilots who were too old for the fighter squadrons or who had failed their powered flight examination, or recruits who had simply never flown before. After theoretical training and intensive flight training on a light glider, they were sent to advance training schools to learn how to fly the CG-4A Waco glider. Towed by C-47s, the pupils learnt to fly in formation as well as landing with full loads, by day and by night, as accurately as possible. They were also taught how to distribute the load inside the glider without unbalancing it as well as how to unload it as quickly as possible. As they had to land behind enemy lines, they received infantry training: hand to hand combat, the use of light weapons, etc. They had orders to reach friendly lines as quickly as possible once their mission was over, in order to be repatriated for further operations.

At the end of their course, trainees became glider pilots and were awarded their wings with the rank of Flight Officer. Often looked down upon by their comrades who piloted powered aircraft, the Glider Pilots nevertheless showed great courage on 6 June 1944 trying to land their heavy gliders by night in closed in hedge-lined fields scattered with 'Rommel's Asparagus.'

A Waco glider pilot shortly before take-off for Normandy. 5 June 1944. The uniform is identical to the glider-borne troops': field jacket, serge trousers, service shoes and leggings. Only the AN-6530 goggles on the helmet, the winged propeller officer insignia on the shirt collar and the USAAF patch on the shoulder tell him apart. The large waxed cloth identification flag (a cut-out armband) is most often seen on glider pilots. The B-3 Life Preserver differs from the B-4 by the leather patch on the front. The M3 lightweight gas mask is carried in the M6 bag. Note the M-1936 belt suspenders, and the Parachute first aid pocket often provided to assault troops. The leather gloves are the regulation issue for officers. Armament includes the M1 Rifle (its clips are contained in the M-1923 cartridge belt), the M1 rifle bayonet (right) and the M3 fighting knife (left). The M-1910 shovel hangs on the right-hand side. Once the glider landed, the pilot became an infantryman until he could make it back to Allied lines. (Another glider pilot silhouette is illustrated on page 75) (Reconstruction)

A cartoon drawn by Dale Oliver, a Waco pilot who took part in Operation Neptune (7 June).

Below.
Unlike their British opposite numbers in the Glider Pilot Regiment which were part of the Army and who took part in the fighting after landing, American glider pilots were part of the US Army Air Forces, and wore its insignia: USAAF patch on the left shoulder, and wing and propeller officer insignia on the shirt collar.
Although they were equipped like infantrymen in case they could not be evacuated, glider pilots had to be taken out of the fighting as soon as the battle situation allowed. Before boarding the boat for Britain, these pilots are commenting their extraordinary adventure and their strained smiles suggest that everything did not necessarily go 'like clockwork!'
Note on the left-hand paratrooper the large-size US flag. The man next to him is leaning on a German k98 rifle which he has brought back as a souvenir: that particular weapon is perhaps nowadays hanging above the mantelpiece of some Texas or Arkansas ranch.
(National Archives)

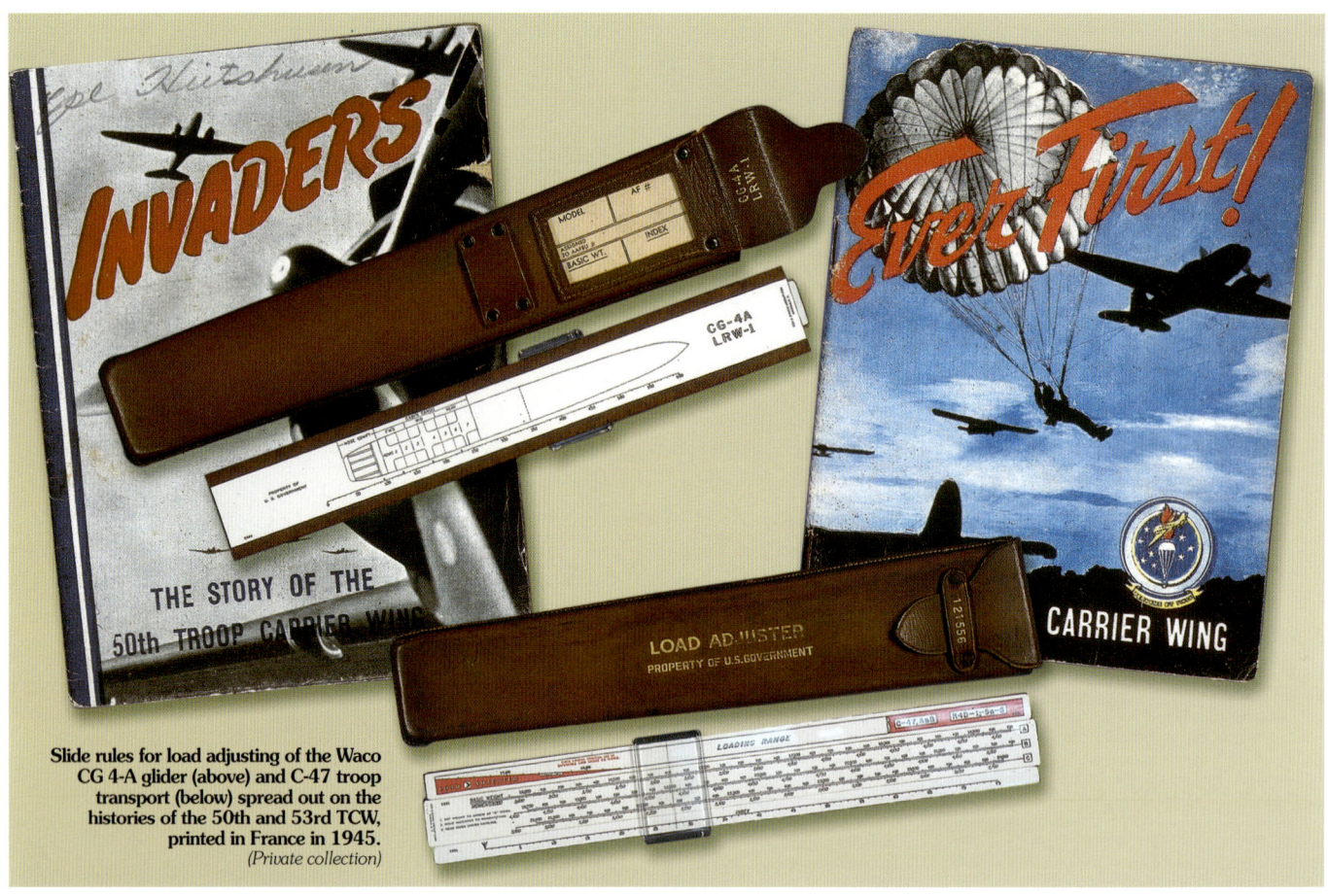

Slide rules for load adjusting of the Waco CG 4-A glider (above) and C-47 troop transport (below) spread out on the histories of the 50th and 53rd TCW, printed in France in 1945.
(Private collection)

Mission accomplished, these glider pilots have piled into an LCVP before boarding a larger ship bound for England. Their tired looks and closed faces are eloquent: the landings were hard, the fighting violent and the losses heavy. On the left, smoking a cigarette, a pilot is wearing the one piece herringbone twill suit under the field jacket. On his left another has kept his AN-6530 goggles.
(National Archives)

CHAPTER 3 OPERATION 'NEPTUNE'

Above.
In the evening of 5 June at the Exeter airfield, 'Screaming Eagles' of the 3rd Battalion, 506th PIR (101st A/B div.) are moving off to their C-47s.
M1 rifles are carried over the shoulder, dismantled in a padded case; the rest of the gear is carried according to one's taste. The third paratrooper from the left has hooked his pistol holster on the left side, which was probably the last free spot on the belt.
The C-47 Skytrooper in the background is the flight leader's for the 440th Troop Carrier Group, 98th Squadron. The radome of the SCR-717 radar can be seen under the fuselage.
The morale of these smiling paratroopers is at its peak and the unbearable stress they have been under during the previous days' long wait was at last over. These men had endured months of intensive training, and the coiled spring of energy and violence would at last be released. The pub brawls with tables and chairs involving His Majesty's Royal Marines and the sometimes fatal riots with the colored soldiers of the Quartermaster Corps were things of the past. The paras would now come to grips with the ever fearsome German Army, which had brought most of Europe to its knees.
This time would be 'the real thing' and there would be no MPs to separate the brawlers!
(National Archives)

The invasion of occupied North-West Europe by the Allied forces under the high command of General Eisenhower was without doubt the largest military operation ever undertaken. Under the codename of 'Overlord,' the action of naval, land and air forces was co-ordinated for the landings. The attack on the eastern coast of the Cotentin Peninsula was carried out by the American VII Corps under General Joseph L. Collins. The 82nd and 101st Airborne Divisions were the airborne element of the attack. Four divisions came by sea; the first was the 4th Infantry Division which landed at Utah. The mission of the VII Corps was to cut the base of the Peninsula and to capture the port of Cherbourg. The airborne divisions covered the landing operations by blocking any attempt to counter-attack by the Germans.

'Overlord' was postponed once on 4 June 1944 in the evening because of the bad weather. On the following day, the weather conditions had been expected to improve and General Eisenhower decided to launch the attack.

Flying in the troops

During the afternoon of 5 June 1944, all the C-47s, and Waco and Horsa gliders of IX Troop Carrier Group were assembled on 14 airfields situated between Lincolnshire and Devon, their crews ready to set off on the great adventure. Towards the end of the day, service vehicles turned up and delivered thousands of cans of paint near the aircraft; they were for painting black and white 'invasion' identification stripes on the wings and fuselage. The orders were very clear: any aircraft operating without these recognition stripes was to be considered as an enemy and shot down. Ground crews and aviators all volunteered for the task of painting all the planes before departure. Even brooms were used to paint the stripes to save time. At 21.30, a C-47 took off from North Witham airfield, piloted by Colonel L. Crouch. It was one of the eleven planes flying in the Pathfinders of the 101st Airborne. At 22.30, the nine planes flying in the Pathfinders from the 82nd Airborne took off. Their mission was to mark out the drop zones for the paratroopers and the landing zones for the gliders half an hour before the first wave arrived.

At 22.48, the first C-47 of this immense armada took off from Greenham Common, piloted by Colonel John M. Donaldson, commanding the 438th Troop Carrier Group. The planes took off at eleven-second intervals. The first planes of the 53rd and 50th Wings were in the air with the paratroopers of the 101st Airborne. They were followed by those of the 52nd Wing carrying the 82nd Airborne. The 821 C-47s assembled at 10 000ft over 'Flatbush,' the radio point situated on the coast at Portland Bill. A 10-mile wide corridor had been planned for air traffic. Altitude was then reduced to 650 ft and all lights were extinguished. The mass of aircraft headed south over the Channel to 'Gallup' point, indicated by a beacon ship of the Royal Navy. Then, near Cherbourg to the west, at 'Hoboken' point, indicated by a luminous signal from a submarine, the planes veered left, climbed to 1,650 feet to avoid the Flak guns on the Channel Islands (Jersey, Guernsey and Alderney), reached the 'Muleshoe' point on the edge of the Normandy Coast. The planes were heading now towards their drop zones. They were flying at 650 feet and they reduced their speed to 110 mph for the drop. Each group of planes was led by two crews who had been trained at the Pathfinder School; these aircraft were equipped with a 'Rebecca' radar set whose continuous signal was set to that of the 'Eureka' beacon switched on the Pathfinders on the ground, thus guiding the planes towards their objective in spite of the dark. Seven holophane lamps set out in the form of a 'T' also showed the direction and the drop point in the drop zone. The first 101st paratroopers were dropped at 00.50 four miles behind Utah Beach and those from the 82nd at 01.50 to the west of Sainte-Mère-Eglise. The aircraft then returned, cutting across the tip of the Cotentin peninsula to the east. The 'Paducah' and 'Spokane' radio points directed them back to 'Gallup' point again where they took up the same corridor as for the outward trip.

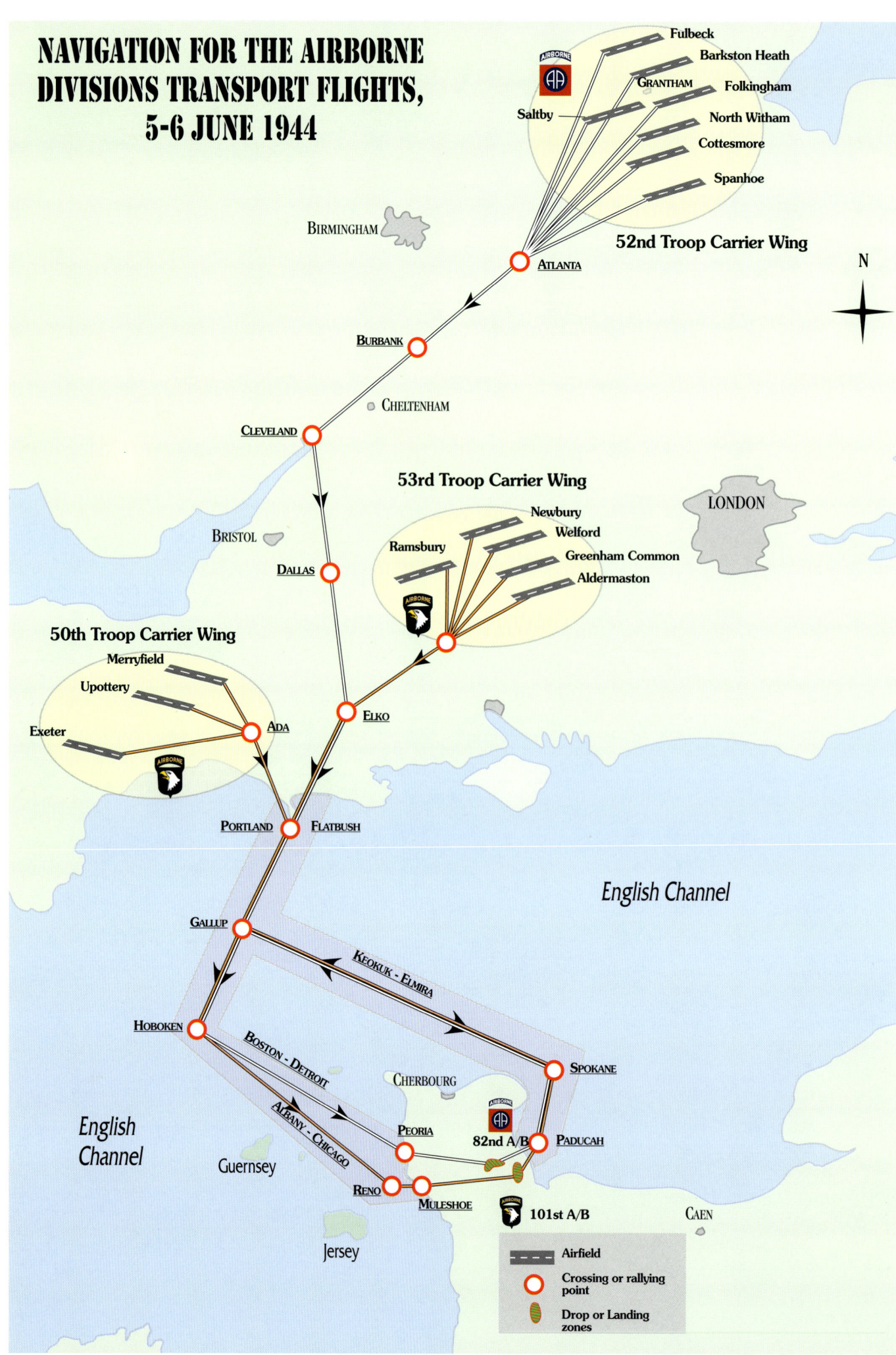

Marking the DZs and the LZs

On the run-in to the Drop Zones, the C-47s carrying the Pathfinders had their approach complicated by banks of clouds and fog appearing over the ground; the pilots were also hampered by the Flak and all this altered the speed, altitude and direction of the planes.

When the drop was made, most sticks were dispersed, sometimes a long way from their targets and part of the marking equipment was lost or destroyed on landing.

The 101st Airborne's sector

Pathfinder teams from the 502nd PIR commanded by Captain Lillyman fell near Saint-Germain de Varreville, one and a quarter mile from DZ 'A.' They managed to set up their marking equipment quickly.

A stick of 506th PIR fell near Drop Zone 'C,' to the north of Hiesville, and marked out the target correctly.

The Pathfinders of the 501st PIR landed at Saint-Côme du Mont to the north of DZ 'D' in areas held by the Germans and had to fight for it. Half of the men were captured or killed and only one 'Eureka' beacon was set up. The lamps could not be swtiched on because the enemy was too near.

The 82nd Airborne's sector

The 505th PIR pathfinder teams were dropped on DZ 'O' near Sainte-Mère-Eglise and marked their zone out promptly.

The Pathfinders of the 507th PIR fell to the west of the Merderet (Amfreville) near DZ 'T.' They had to fight the Germans patrolling in the sector. The sticks were dispersed, the lamps lost. Only one Eureka beacon was operational.

The Pathfinders from the 508th PIR fell about one and a half mile to the south-east of DZ 'N' near Pont-l'Abbé. Only one beacon and two holophane lamps could be set up.

Overall the DZ and LZ marking out operations were a failure; this had serious consequences on the following massed drops of the airborne divisions.

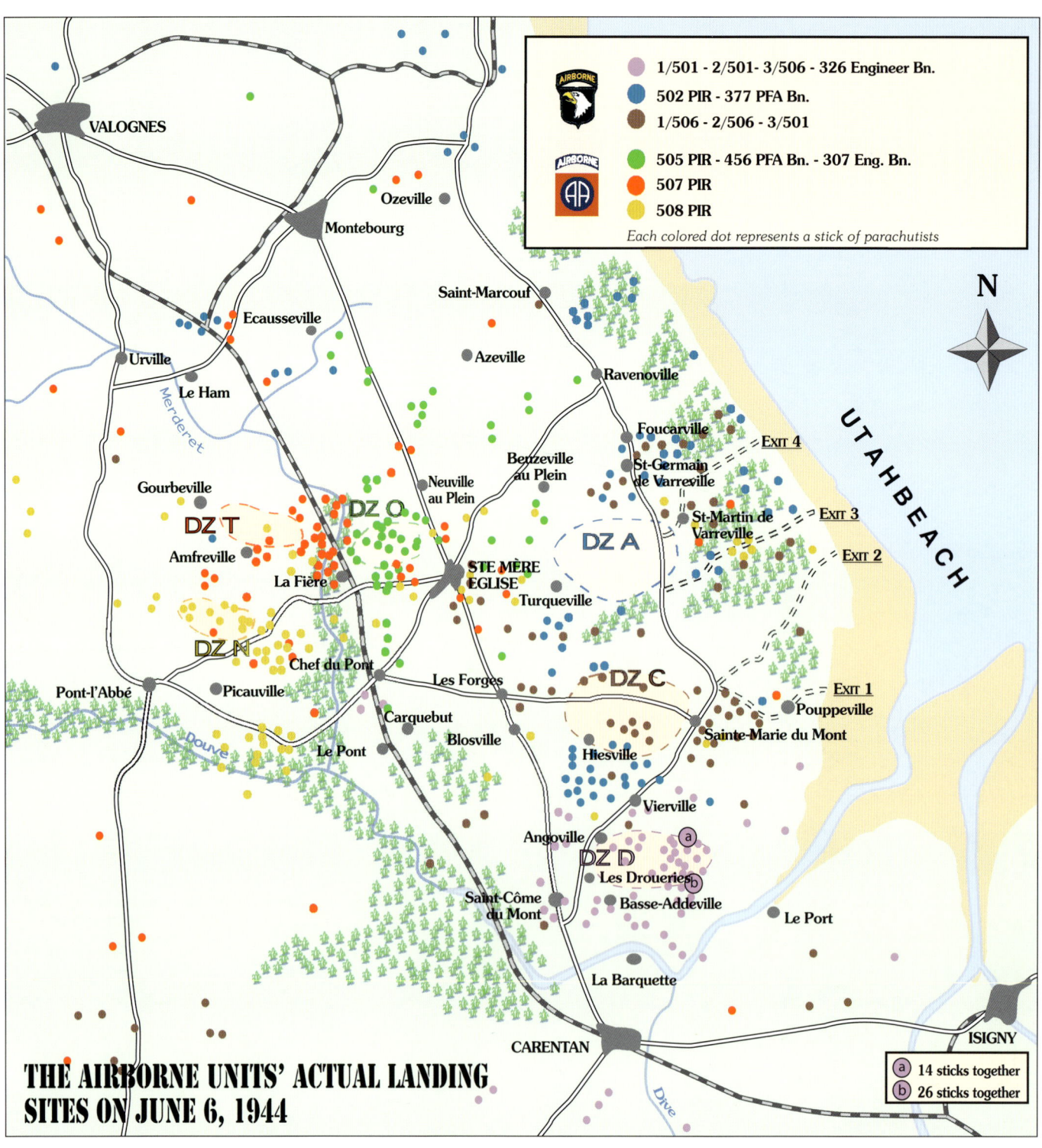

THE AIRBORNE UNITS' ACTUAL LANDING SITES ON JUNE 6, 1944

Note in particular that 2/505 was dropped to the south of DZ 'C' instead of DZ 'A', its assigned objective. The 507th PIR was also widely dispersed: the C-47 pilots, hampered by the Flak, broke formation and dropped their sticks miles from anywhere, some more than twelve or eighteen miles from the DZ.

The missions

The 'Albany' mission was tasked to bring in General Maxwell Taylor's 101st Airborne div. over three dropzones (A, B and C) and one landing zone (E) to the east and south west of Sainte-Mère-Eglise, behind Utah Beach. Their job was to secure the beach exits from Utah and to destroy the German gun batteries at Saint-Martin de Vareville.

2/505 was dropped in bulk to the left of DZ 'C' instead of the initial DZ 'A.' This spot, tightly hemmed-in by hedgerows, made orientation and assembling very difficult. 3/502 was wildly dispersed to the east of Sainte-Mère Eglise. 75 men however managed to reach the Saint-Martin battery, but it had been deserted by its crew, and the guns themselves had been moved away.

Exits 3 and 4 in the northern section of Utah Beach were reached and secured, the junction with the 4th Division took place at 13.00.

The 1st Bn. of the 502d PIR landed near Saint-Germain de Varreville, and heavy fighting took place around Mesières. The battalion then helped with clearing the northern Utah beach exits.

The 506th PIR drop came off slightly better than the others, over DZ 'C' and despite heavy Flak which brought down several Dakotas. But frequent firefights with the Germans prevented the paras from reaching and securing exits 1 (Pouppeville) and 2 (Houdienville). These were captured by the 4th Division in the morning.

The 377th PFABn had the worst luck and only a single howitzer was in firing order.

3/501st was tasked with holding the LZ 'E' perimeter near Hiesville.

General Taylor ordered 40 men to attack the strongpoints near Pouppeville but the Germans, however disorganized, repelled American attacks from more than four hours. Half the paras became casualties and the area was not cleared until the seaborne troops came in.

The 'Boston' Mission had to drop men from General Ridgway's 82nd Airborne over three DZs (O, N and T) and two LZs (O and W) to the west of Sainte-Mère-Eglise. They were to establish a defensive line to the west of the Merderet River, take Sainte-Mère-Eglise, and capture the La Fière and Chef du Pont bridges. The first artillery reinforcement would come in in two glider waves before daybreak.

(Continued on page 34)

THE PATHFINDERS

The first operational jumps made by the 82nd Airborne in North Africa and Sicily (July 1943) resulted in excessive losses because the drops were too scattered or too far from the target.

In order to improve this situation, it was decided to form teams of airborne scouts (Pathfinders), sent in the drop zones in order to reconnoitre them and mark them out before the massed drops.

New equipment such as the 'Eureka' (AN/PPN-1A), the transmitter beacon had just been approved: its use together with 'Rebecca,' the receiver (APN-2) mounted aboard the C-47s greatly improved navigating the transport planes. The first pathfinders (50 men) were successfully used in Italy (13-14 Sept. 1943).

The Pathfinder school was created in February 1944 at North Witham aerodrome, in England. Colonel Joel Crouch of the Army Air Forces was in command of the IX Troop Carrier Command C-47 pathfinder crews which had seen action in Italy. Each of the three parachute regiments of the 82nd and 101st Airborne Divisions had to supply the necessary men to be trained as pathfinders at North Witham with Air Force crews.

Above.
Pathfinder sleeve insignia.

Below.
Carrying bag for the Eureka PPN-1 beacon.
(H-P. Enjames collection, GI Collector Guide)

Lieutenant-Colonel Crouch, commanding the pathfinder planes, and his crew at North Witham on 5 June 1944, a few hours before leaving for Normandy.
From left to right: Ray Culp, navigator; Joel Crouch, pilot; Conrad, radio operator; Vito Pedone, co-pilot; Dr Ed Cannon, flight surgeon E. Larendeal, jumpmaster. Note the various uniforms: A-2 and B-10 flight jackets, A-4 suit, RAF 1941-pattern and American B-4 life-jackets. Crouch is armed with an impressive M-1918 fighting knife.

(Photo J. Crouch, via Jean-Yves Nasse)

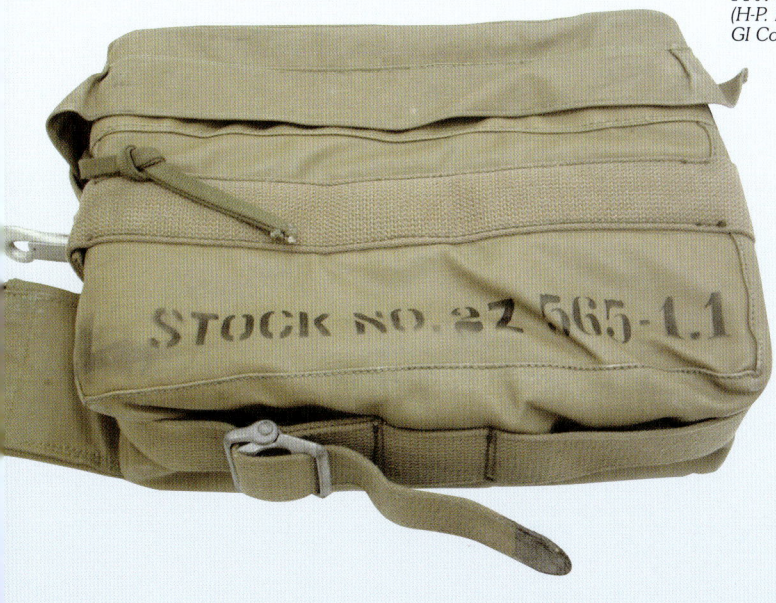

Marking the LZs and DZs

The 'Eureka' beacon was switched on with the frequency set on that of the 'Rebecca' receivers in the planes. Seven holophane lamps were laid out in front of the beacon in the shape of a T. The upright of the T directed the planes towards the DZ and the horizontal bar indicated the beginning of the DZ. To enable the lead ships to find their respective DZs, the zone was indi-

Plane No 1 pathfinder stick from the 1/502 PIR (101st A/B div.), North Witham field, 5 June 1944. Several paratroopers have placed Thompson SMG mag pockets on the M-1936 belt suspenders. The second trooper standing from the left has an M3 'Grease Gun' SMG.
These paras are led by Capt. Lillyman, the 101st pathfinders leader and they will be flown in by Lt.-Col. Crouch, the IX Troop carrier pathfinders leader. Take-off time 22.30, drop over DZ 'A' (Saint-Germain de Varreville) at 00.15.
(DR)

The Pathfinder Team

— 1 officer, team leader
— 1 officer, second-in-command;
— 2 'Eureka' beacon transmitter operators;
— 2 assistant 'Eureka' transmitter operators
— 1 Holophane lamp section commander
— 7 men, with two Holophane lamps each;
— 4-6 men for perimeter security
Total: **18-20 men**
Two each of marking gear was carried for back-up

cated by different colored lamps; for example

DZ O: green (505 PIR)
DZ T: red (507 PIR)
DZ N: Amber (508 PIR)

The last light on the end of the upright was activated by an operator equipped with a key which flashed the letter in Morse, i.e. N for DZ 'N', etc.

Each pathfinder team was 'mated' to a C-47 and its crew. They trained and lived together in symbiosis. The paratroopers were trained in air navigation,

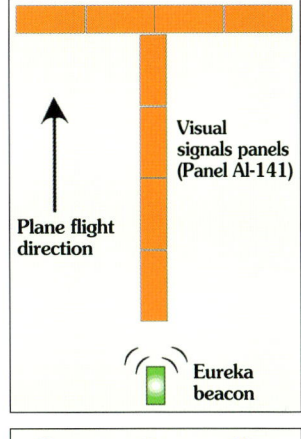

Visual signals panels (Panel Al-141)

Plane flight direction

Eureka beacon

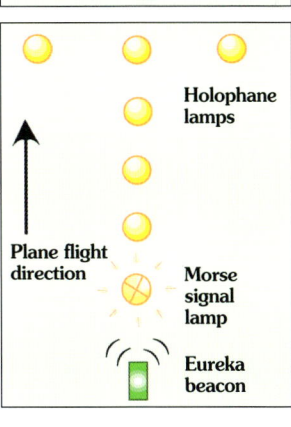

Holophane lamps

Plane flight direction

Morse signal lamp

Eureka beacon

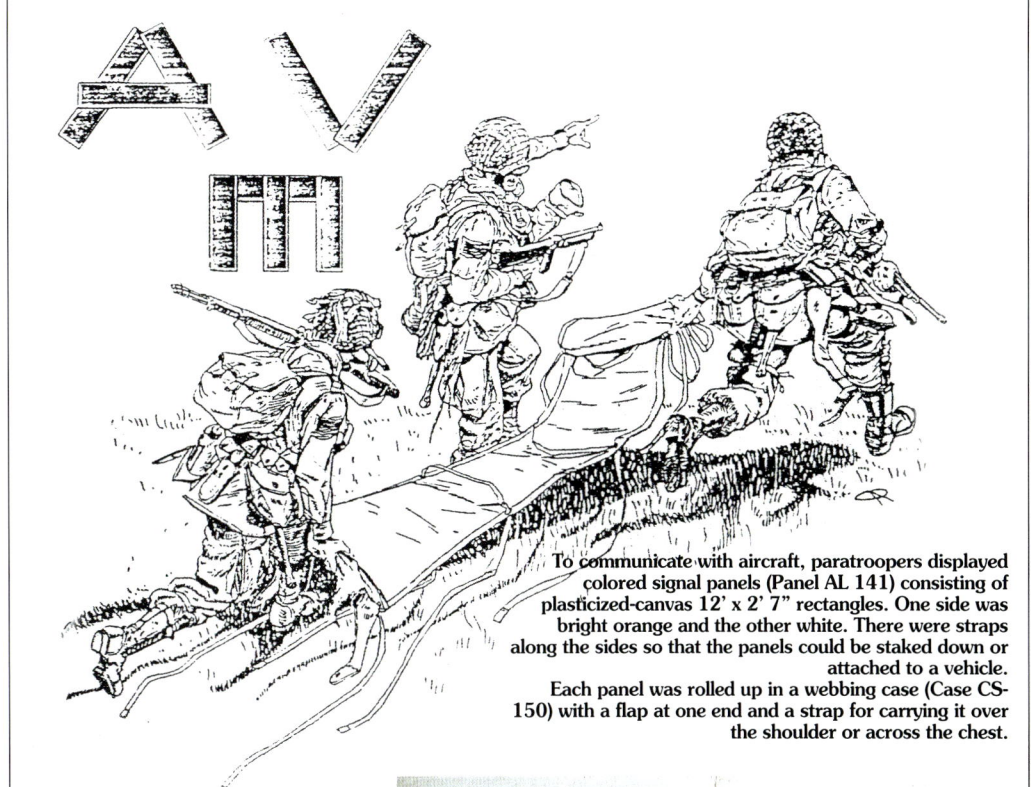

To communicate with aircraft, paratroopers displayed colored signal panels (Panel AL 141) consisting of plasticized-canvas 12' x 2' 7" rectangles. One side was bright orange and the other white. There were straps along the sides so that the panels could be staked down or attached to a vehicle.
Each panel was rolled up in a webbing case (Case CS-150) with a flap at one end and a strap for carrying it over the shoulder or across the chest.

some pilots were qualified parachutists. The plane navigators used conventional calculations to work out the distance and time of arrival over the objective; the 'Rebecca' radars were only used by the lead ships.

The paratrooper pathfinders made 5 to 7 training jumps a week of which two were by night. Calorie-rich meals improved their night vision. During the night of 11 May 1944 during the 'Eagle' exercise, seven Pathfinder teams from the 101st Airborne were dropped; six found the DZs and marked them out 30 minutes before the arrival of the 6,000 paratroopers of the 101st Airborne brought in by 432 planes; the exercise went perfectly. The Pathfinders were now perfectly trained for operation 'Neptune.'

Above.
'Para Map', an air orientation map issued to paratroopers for Operation Neptune. Here, for the Sainte-Marie du Mont sector.

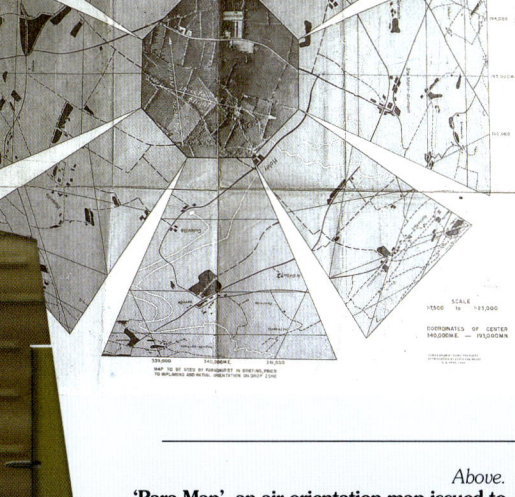

C-47 from the IX Troop Carrier Pathfinder Group

North Witham field, 5 June 1944.
The machine is equipped with both the APN-2 Receiver ('Rebecca') whose characteristic aerial can be seen near the cockpit, and the SCR-717 Radar whose radome is visible under the fuselage. All unit markings have been painted over. The hinges sticking out near the cargo door have been taped over to prevent accidental hitches. On 6 June 1944 at 00.16 this plane dropped Pathfinder Stick No 19 from the 502nd PIR (Lieutenant Don S. Driver) over DZ 'C.'
(Computer graphics by Nicolas Gohin, © Histoire & Collections 2004)

AERIAL MEANS USED FOR THE AIRBORNE OPERATION

● **808 C-47s dropped over the Cotentin Peninsula:**
— 13,110 Parachutists
— 14 Howitzers
— 389 tons of supplies and equipment

● **309 C-47s brought in to the landing zones:**
— 170 Horsa gliders
— 139 Waco gliders
Total
— 1,679 Glider troops
— 215 vehicles
— 75 artillery guns (57-mm antitank guns and 75-mm howitzers)
— 174 tons of supplies and equipment

● **Losses for D-Day**
– 28 C-47s destroyed
– 334 C-47s damaged
– 101 crew members killed, wounded or missing
– 53 glider pilots killed or wounded on landing
– 258 glider troops killed or wounded on landing.

A short while after D-Day, the 'Screaming Eagles' joined up with the sea-borne troops which had landed on Utah Beach, as can be seen from the GMC truck in the background. The MPs are already controlling traffic. The early road congestion seems to have subsided. Even if the enemy is still near, the faces no longer bear the signs of anguish. But fierce fighting in the Norman 'bocage' is just round the corner for these paratroopers of 506 PIR.
The jeep in the foreground, which had probably been airlifted by the Horsa glider in background, is towing a light infantry trailer (Hand cart M3A4) loaded with an aerial delivery A-5 Container. The driver has placed his M1 Rifle within reach in the leather holster 'Scabbard Rifle, 1938 Model.'
(National Archives)

(Continued from page 30)

The 82nd A/B div. drop was very widely dispersed. Only one regiment succeeded in carrying out its designated mission. 180 paratroopers from the 3rd Battalion of the 505th PIR (Lt. Col. Krause) captured Sainte-Mère-Eglise at around 04.30. Most of the Germans there belonged to a Flak supply column which had left the village a short while before the drop started. The paratroopers of the 2/505 PIR under Lt. Col. Vandervoort fought the Germans which counter-attacked to the south of Sainte-Mère-Eglise. Towards 10.00, the Georgians from Ost-Bataillon 795 and the Germans from the 91st Luftlande Division attacked with a few Stug III self-propelled guns. They were driven off by 3/505 who destroyed a retreating German convoy with grenades. The mission of the 1/505 was to capture the bridge at La Fière over the River Merderet. But they were stopped by German machine gun fire; the paratroopers of the 2nd Batallion, 507th PIR took part in the action. The La Fière sector was only secured after three days. The two other regiments (507th and 508th PIR) dropped on the west bank of the River Merderet and were widely spread out (the Pathfinders had not been able to mark out the zone properly because of enemy action). Many paratroopers fell into the flooded marshes as did a good part of the equipment. The only high point in this area was the Caen-Cherbourg railway line.

The 'Chicago' Mission included 52 Waco gliders transporting 155 men from the 101st Airborne as well as 57-mm anti-tank guns, jeeps and their trailers, a light bulldozer and tons of ammunition and equipment to a landing zone situated 2 miles to the south of Sainte-Mère-Eglise. The first glider landed at 03.54 with General Pratt on board; but it crashed into a tree, killing the general and breaking both legs of the pilot, Mike Murphy.

The 'Detroit' Mission included 52 gliders carrying 220 men from the 82nd Airborne and their equipment, between 04.00 and 04.10, to a LZ situated to the north of Sainte-Mère-Eglise.

Only 17 pilots landed their gliders within the landing zone or even near it. Fourteen pilots and glider troops lost their lives. The main cause was the lack of visibility which prevented them from seeing the trees and the hedges.

'Keokuk' was a reinforcement mission for the 101st Airborne and took place on the evening of 6 June, at 20.53. Thirty two heavily-laden Horsa gliders were released over the landing zone situated to the west of Hiesville. They carried 160 Signal, Medical and Headquarters personnel, 40 vehicles, 6 artillery guns and 19 tons of ammunition, as well as elements from the 327 GIR. Two gliders landed behind the German lines; there were 14 killed and 30 wounded.

'Elmira' was a reinforcement mission for the 82nd Airborne. Its landing zone, LZW, was situated to the south of Sainte-Mère-Eglise (Les

Forges).

It consisted of two phases. The first was made up of a wave of 8 Waco and 18 Horsa gliders, followed by a second of 14 Waco and 36 Horsa gliders carrying 438 men, 64 jeeps, 13 anti-tank guns, 24 tons of medical equipment and ammunition to LZ 'W' at 21.04. The German held part of the landing zone and General Ridgway tried in vain to divert it elsewhere. The glider pilots had to land in small hedge-lined fields scattered with 'Rommel's asparagus.' Half the Wacos were damaged or destroyed as well as 80% of the Horsas. Five glider pilots were killed, four went missing and 17 were wounded.

In the second phase of 'Elmira,' 86 Horsa and 14 Wacos took in men and equipment from the 319th and 320th Glider Field Artillery Battalions as well as elements of the 307th Medical Company. The Flak was very heavy and night was falling when the machines reached the Landing Zone at 23.00. The pilots had to land their gliders in fields scattered with tall trees and surrounded by hedges.

50 Horsas were destroyed and all the Wacos were either damaged or destroyed. Out of 196 crewmen, 10 were killed and 29 wounded. Out of the 737 glider troops belonging to the 82nd Airborne, 28 were killed and 106 wounded.

At midnight on 6 June, only 4,500 paratroopers out of 13,500 were under the command of their own division, 10% only having actually landed on the planned DZs.

Even though most German units stationed in the airborne attack sectors were 'second rate' (Russians, Poles, etc.), the paratroopers were too widely spread out and had a lot of trouble reaching their targets. In spite of this, the Germans were totally confused; they were unable to evaluate the situation and the enemy strength properly. They were therefore unable to counter-attack effectively. This airborne assault by night turned out to be a partial failure and was not repeated again in later operations.

Evaluating the airborne units' casualties on the evening of 6 June is impossible: one can understand that at the heart of the battle, with the large number of stray soldiers, the officers had other things on their minds than take roll call!

Considering that the 82nd A/B was only relieved on 8 July and that the 101st, after capturing Carentan, had to fight off a counter-attack by the 17th SS Division and the 6.Fallschirmjäger-Regt., the total losses at the end of the campaign (including killed, wounded and missing) were calculated as follows:

The 'Missing' column causes a certain amount of confusion because it includes the men who strayed far from the jump zone and who joined up much later, as well as those taken prisoner, and of course those who remain forever trapped in the muddy waters of the Rivers Dives and Merderet…

82nd and 101st Airborne Divisions Casualties

DIVISION	KILLED	WOUNDED	MISSING	TOTAL
82nd Airborne	457	1,440	2,571	4,468
101st Airborne	546	2,217	1,907	4,670

The losses suffered by the two airborne divisions on D-Day were nevertheless lower than the estimates. General Eisenhower had in fact been told that the losses would amount to between 50 and 80% …

Landing skid from a Waco CG-4A glider found in the Les Forges sector. (LZ 'W')

The first gliders land…

(George E. Buckley via Jean-Yves Nasse)

George E. Buckley, a Waco glider pilot in the 74th Troop Carrier Squadron of the 434th Group based at Aldermaston recalls:

"My group was part of the first gliders to land in Normandy on 6 June 1944. I was flying No 9 glider and in front of me was No 1 glider in which General Pratt was killed on landing. It was 4 AM and totally dark.

There were 50 gliders landing on LZ 'E' (Hiesville) and we were carrying elements of the 101st Airborne, anti-tank guns, jeeps, medical teams, rations and ammunition, everything that was too heavy to be parachuted.

At daybreak, the German tanks and self-propelled guns gave us a hard time. The guns we were carrying were going to come in handy. My glider carried one with its crew of artillerymen from the 81st AAABn. On landing we crashed because of the dark, but everybody was safe and sound. We succeeded in getting the gun out of the wrecked glider with the help of a jeep from a CG-4A which had landed nearby. 45 minutes later, it went into action.

My glider was nicknamed 'Jeannebelle'."

Horsa Glider control wheel, recovered in the vicinity of Sainte-Mère-Eglise.

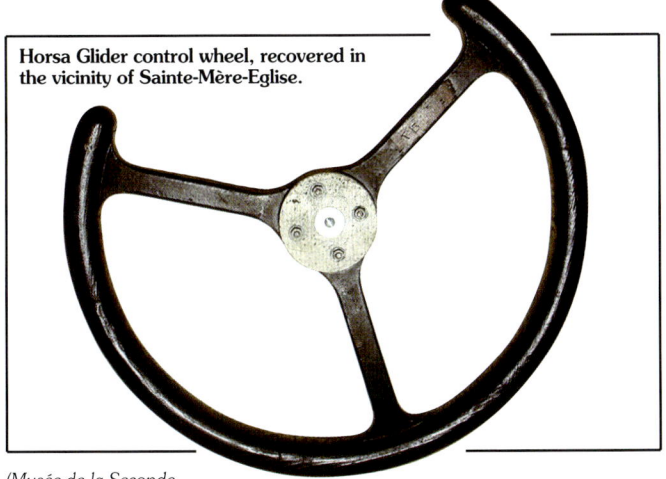

(Musée de la Seconde Guerre mondiale at Ambleteuse, Pas-de-Calais)

A paratrooper from the 505th PIR (82nd Airborne div.), exhausted by the fighting, in the ruins of Saint-Sauveur le Vicomte.
Note the belt suspender straps wound with tape to protect the shoulders.
A spoon, slipped into the breast pocket, is within easy reach. Although damaged, the thin cotton flag is still in place on the right arm.
The fine-mesh camouflage netting on the helmet was typical of this division.
(Photo R. Capa, collection of the International center of photography, New York)

(Reconstruction, photo Pierre Schubert)

CHAPTER 4 THE JUMP SUIT

Shortly before and early in the war, the Quartermaster Corps defined a new standard combat uniform, around the modern-looking 'Jacket Field,' adopted in 1941. But, at their request, the QMC also started work on additional 'specialized' uniforms for new arms such as armor crews and parachutists, for whom the standard issue would not be suitable.

Indeed the paratroopers needed completely different clothing which would be better suited to their mission. What they did not like particularly with the field jacket and wool trouser combination was the lack of large-capacity pockets.

Combat and jump dress

The apparently strong desire for a specific uniform was motivated by the spirit of individuality at all costs, not uncommon in certain elite corps. Furthermore there was already a trend for specialized clothing depending on the type of combat, terrain or climate; and the paratroopers got what they wanted.

In 1941, after eliminating a one-piece coverall which was practical for jumping but not for combat, the first two-piece prototype uniform was shown to officers of the newly established parachute units.

After a few modifications, particularly where fastening the pockets was concerned, the definitive version was approved in December 1941, with the designation 'Coat, Parachute Jumper.' The jump trousers were in turn approved early in 1942, under the designation 'Trousers, Parachute Jumper.' This combination of trousers and jacket would be known afterwards among collectors as the '1942 Jump Suit.'

Jump dress

Coat, Parachute Jumper
Stock number 55-C-35808/55-C-35862

Made of Olive Drab Shade No 2 cotton poplin, the coat was in the form of a jacket with four pockets, taken in at the waist. The garment was unlined. The pockets gave the jacket its characteristic shape. Their volume was increased depending on what was put in them thanks to side bellows and a vertical gusset. The flaps could be attached in two positions thanks to two sets of 'male' snaps. These press studs bore the markings 'Durable' or 'Scovill' and were made of black painted metal or chemically tarnished brass.

Depending on the makers, the two breast pockets were slightly slanted to allow easier access for the hands. The jacket was closed by means of a zip fastener under a flap, and a light belt with a prongless metal buckle. Below the collar there was a small vertical pocket, accessible by means of two zip fasteners, used for holding the M2 switchblade knife. The bottom of the sleeves had a small vent which was closed with two snaps. Under the armpits, there were four ventilation holes with painted metal grommets or finished with stitches. A white cloth label sewn inside the lower right-hand pocket bore the following information:
- Coat, Parachute Jumper
- Maker's name
- Contract number
- Date of the contract
– Quartermaster specification
- Date of specification
- Stock Number
- Size
- Phila. Quartermaster Depot
- Inspector

The size was marked in black ink inside the back of the jacket (i.e. 38R)

Ease of movement and volume were obtained from three wide pleats on the back: two from the shoulder to the waist and the third in the center, taken in at the waist and gong down to the bottom. The jacket was worn over the standard woolen shirt and the 'Sweater Highneck,' if taken.

The makes of zip fasteners used on the Jump coats were Crown, Talon, Conmar and Serval.

Trousers, Parachute Jumper
Stock number 55-TC-40499/55-T-50563

These were tailored using the same cloth as the coat with the same principles of practicality, with two large pockets on the thighs going down to the knee. The details were the same with gussets, and asymmetrical flaps fastened by press studs.

Apart from the cargo pockets, there was a small gusset on the front right-hand side, two regular slightly slanted pockets ands two hip pock-

(Continued on page 40)

THE JUMI

Left, and opposite page.
These two paratroopers are wearing brand new non-reinforced jump suits.

A. This Technician 4th Grade of the 101st A/B div. is wearing a skull cap, a non-regulation knit item which sometimes replaced the M-1941 issue knit cap ('Beanie'). Note the characteristic shape of the cargo pockets on the trousers. The woolen shirt is the standard issue, worn with a camo scarf cut from a parachute canopy.

B. This view clearly shows the baggy cut of the trousers above the jump boots, these being brand new as well. The braces were indispensable for the trousers not to slip down under the weight of all the accessories stuffed into the pockets.

C. This Private from the 82nd Div. has probably just come out of the supply room and is smugly wearing his impeccable uniform. The differences in shade between the trousers and jacket can be explained by the slightly different dye baths used by cloth makers. As both items are mint, they have kept their original shade. Note that, along the stitching on the chest pocket flaps, there is a narrow slit for a pencil, the spoon of a grenade or the clip of the angled-head TL 122 lamp.
(Reconstruction, photo Militaria Magazine)

SUIT

Above.
Early on the morning of 6 June after the hard fighting during the night near Sainte-Mère-Eglise, this paratrooper tries to rest for a moment. The chincup and straps have been slipped inside the helmet liner. The flag armband, typical of the 82nd Airborne Division, is sewn at the top of the right sleeve. The trousers reinforcing patches are clearly visible on the knees as well as the bellows of the cargo pockets. These are filled to bursting. A British Hawkins anti-tank mine is tied to the calf.
(Reconstruction)

D. The pleats on the back and the vent at the bottom of the skirt of the jacket are clearly shown here. The method of fastening the wristbands with two press studs is characteristic, the same system being used on the collar. The shoulder straps are held near the collar by a press stud.
(Reconstruction)

Left.
1943, Camp Mackall (North Carolina). These two paratroopers pose proudly in their pristine jump suits. On the left, Tom Porcella (508th PIR), who has given us numerous eye-witness accounts, is already wearing paratroopers wings pinned above the left-hand breast pocket.
(Tom Porcella)

Below.
**Night has fallen on 5 June and the paratroopers of the 506th PIR (101st A/B div.) are climbing into their designated C-47. The men are literally crushed by the weight of their equipment, as shown here clearly and the crew have to help them up into the plane.
The paratrooper at right, his face blackened, has strapped the M-1936 musette bag under the parachute chest pack, and apparently his assault gas mask under that.
On the left the pilot, wearing a wool homemade sweater, leggings and a life jacket, is smoking a last cigarette before take-off.**
(National Archives)

ets without flaps. The left pocket was shut by means of a bakelite button, exactly the same as those of the fly and braces.

The trousers were slightly tapered towards the bottom in such a way as to slip into the tops of the jump boots without needing to be folded. The pocket linings and inside reinforcements were made of strong off-white cloth used for lining most service pants. The jump trousers were worn with braces and the standard webbing belt. Very often they were worn over the regulation woolen trousers for warmth.

An over-fragile uniform

Production was started immediately and the new suit got its baptism of fire in North Africa during Operation 'Torch' in November 1942. It was without doubt very practical but the material was not sturdy enough - as well as being to light in shade - and it turned out to be much too fragile for the type of missions which paratroopers took part in. The knees and the elbows wore through too quickly and the cargo pockets, stuffed full of all sorts of items got torn easily.

So at the end of 1943, when the paratroopers of the 82nd Airborne were billeted in England after their turn of duty in the Mediterranean theatre of operations, everything was done to improve the existing uniforms. At that moment, the M-1943 combat uniform had not yet been issued and the 1942 suit had therefore to be made more resistant in the meantime.

Above.
Inside a C-47 cabin at the Upottery airfield. These men of the 506th PIR (101st A/B div.) are receiving a last briefing before the off. The officer standing with binoculars by his side is wearing his escape map (a map of Normandy printed on cotton) tied round his neck. An extra pocket taken from a reclaimed jump suit has been sewn onto the left sleeve. The brown and green strips of jute in the helmet netting are the type used by the British Army.
(National Archives)

Reinforced Jump Suits

A systematic analysis of photographs taken of the Normandy Campaign does in fact show that in the majority of cases, US Paratroopers wore reinforced uniforms. The jackets had sewn-on reinforcing patches on the elbows and the bellows of the pockets; on the trousers, they were placed on the weak spots: the knees and the cargo pockets side bellows. Two straps intended to compress the pockets when they were full were included in the inseam leg stitching or simply sewn flat along a few inches.

The patches themselves were made of canvas scraps whose colors varied from dark olive green to dirty gray, mainly due to washing and the anti-gas impregnation.

A survey of surviving uniforms in several private collections proves that the patches were applied after the clothes had been made in the factory. The trouser legs and jacket sleeves had been unstitched in order to slip the reinforcing patches inside and then re-stitched, often very roughly, with different thread from that used by the makers. As for the probable date of the modifications, photographs showing paratroopers manoeuvering in the USA then in England in March to April 1944 only show non-reinforced uniforms.

One may conclude therefore that the modifications were made urgently a short while before 5 June by the parachute maintenance and repair (riggers) workshops of the Airborne Divisions.

Although the majority of uniforms had been reinforced by D-Day, some of the period photographs show un-modified uniforms.

After several weeks' fighting, the jump suits were almost in shreds, and just before the paratroopers shipped for England, they were taken way and replaced with brand-new fatigues (Account by Tom Porcella, 508th PIR).

Major Edward C. Krause, nicknamed 'Cannonball,' the commanding officer of the 3rd Battalion of the 505th, 82nd A/B div., got hold of Sainte-Mère-Eglise during the night of 6 June 1944. Only the rank insignia painted on the front of his helmet distinguishes him from an enlisted man. The jump suit, all crumpled up, is also misshapen by the weight of the very heavily-laden pockets.
(Photo Derick Wills, DR)

41

The reinforced jump suit belonged to Private Elmer F. Schein (Army serial number 13039070) of the 502nd PIR of the 101st A/B div., who died of his wounds on 3 July 1944 and who was buried in the American cemetery at Cambridge in England. The straps on the trouser pockets have been made with the flat webbing typical of this division.

The helmet is the standard M1 combined with a (Westinghouse-made) paratrooper liner, a common practice. The medium-mesh netting garnished with jute cloth strips (typical of the 101st A/B) hides the 'White Hearts' of the 502nd PIR painted on both sides of the helmet.

The 'Rigger Made' ammunition pockets inspired by the Airforce issue ('Holder Rifle Clip') contained clips for the M1 Rifle, or Mk II frag. grenades.

The M-1910 shovel with shortened handle is worn on the left hip. The M-1910 canteen is carried inside the 'Cover, Canteen, Mounted M-1941' which was more resistant than the standard pattern. The bag ('Bag, Canvas, Field, OD, M-1936') used by all paratroopers hangs from the 'Suspenders, Belt, M1936', which are lined with felt padding on the shoulders.

Paratrooper from the 502nd PIR, Sainte-Marie du Mont. 6 June 1944 in the morning

The M-1911A1 automatic pistol in its brown leather holster (M-1916) is attached to the standard belt (Belt, Pistol, M-1936). The M1 bayonet is fixed to the rifle barrel.
The brass cricket, used only by the 101st A/B div., is hanging from the neck by a length of string. The M3 knife in its leather M6 scabbard is strapped to the calf. Note the characteristic toe cap of the Jump Boots ('Boots, Jumper, Parachute').
(Reconstruction)

43

PARATROOP OFFICERS

Above.
An 82nd airborne div. officer
The arm-of-service insignia pinned to the shirt collar (two crossed rifles) singles him out as an infantry officer. He is armed with an M1A1 folding stock carbine. The M-1938 despatch (map) case holder and M3 binoculars were also part of an officer's gear. The parachute first aid pocket is tied to the webbing suspenders. Note the heavy-duty cloth patches on the jacket elbows, the trouser knees and the bellows of the trouser pockets.
(Reconstruction)

This other view of the 502d PIR paratrooper (previous page) shows the British gas detection armband on the right shoulder, which was very common in the 101st A/B div. The M5 gas mask is in its rubber M7 bag strapped onto the waist and thigh. The gloves are the mounted troop model. A bandoleer containing clips for the M1 Rifle is worn across the chest. The parachute first aid pocket is knotted on the left suspender belt.
(Reconstruction)

On the jump jacket and trousers, the elbows, the pocket bellows and knees have been reinforced with heavy cloth. The straps for tightening the pockets are made from the same material as the patches, a typically 82nd A/B design. The fine-mesh helmet netting was also typical of the unit. The plastic wrist compass, a general issue item, has been tied to the pistol belt. The M3 fighting knife in its plastic M8 sheath is placed on the right leg, held by a leather thong and a strap salvaged from unserviceable webbing gear.

This officer has the regulation issue weapon, an M1A1 folding stock carbine, and an additional M-1911A1 pistol. The lightweight carbine was often traded for a Thompson sub-machine gun or the M1 Rifle. The Parachute First Aid Packet has been tied to the left webbing suspender strap.
Our officer is carrying the same gear as enlisted men, such as the folding M-1943 shovel as well as a locally-made box-shaped ammunition pouch in the back.
No rank insignia are worn.
(Reconstruction)

82nd Airborne Division officer

45

The camouflaged Jump Jacket

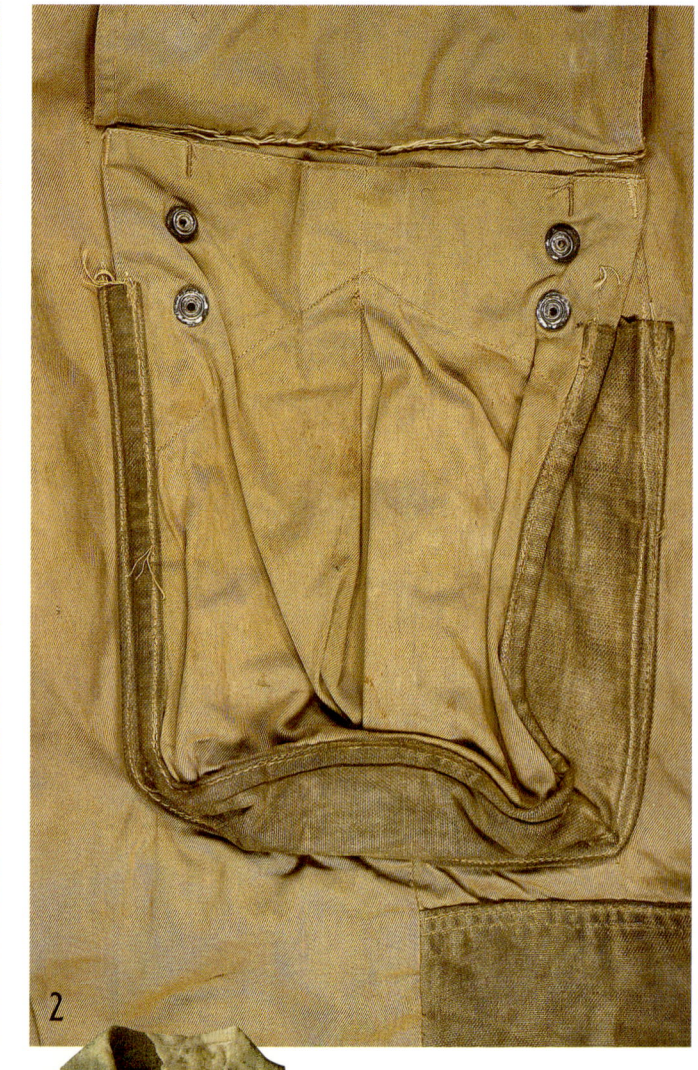

This magnificent jump jacket, a relic of D-Day, comes from the Montebourg region. The camouflage pattern was brushed in two shades of green and very effectively breaks the original tan color hardly suitable for operations in Normandy. This practice was particularly common with the Pathfinders. The gas detection arm band is still in place. The pockets and elbows (invisible here) have been reinforced. The jacket has been impregnated with a gas-proofing compound (CC-2, Chloroamid) which gave it a unpleasant, tacky feel to the touch. The name of the paratrooper NCO 'R. E Odon,' has been stenciled on an improvised name tape. The insignia of the 101st AB div. has come unstitched and has left its tell-tale mark. The First Sergeant's stripes have not been spared by the camouflage daubing. RE Odon belonged to HQ Battery of the 377th PFABn.
(Musée Mémorial d'Omaha Beach)

1. The reinforcement on the knee of 101st A/B jump trousers.
2. Thigh pocket bellow reinforcement on 101st A/B trousers.
3. Tightening strap on 101st A/B trousers. The flat strap has been let into the seam of the trousers.
4. Typical positioning of the pocket straps on 82nd Airborne div. jump suit trousers. The strap was made from the same cloth as the reinforcements on the knees and the pockets.
(Private collection and Musée de la Seconde Guerre Mondiale at Ambleteuse)

A paratrooper from the 82nd Airborne Division at Sainte-Mère-Eglise. His helmet is covered with the fine-mesh netting typical of this division. He has hooked Mk II fragmentation grenades into the slits of the chest pocket flaps
(National Archives)

47

THE JUMP BOOTS

From 1940 onwards, following trials carried out at Fort Benning by the Parachute test platoon, the Infantry Board of the QMC which looked after equipment for the airborne troops, decided that boots were the most important item of the Jump uniform. Two types of boots which already existed were analyzed: the German paratroopers' lace-up boots with rubber soles and those belonging to the firemen of the US Forest Service which have a strap and buckle on the instep. Several prototypes which took up the best elements of these shoes were made and tested by the 501st Parachute Battalion and the 502nd PIR between January 1941 and July 1942. Several modifications were made before the final model was found then approved on 2 August 1942 under the designation 'Boots, Parachute Jumper' (Quartermaster specification BQD No 58D, August 3, 1942). The specification was issued by the Boston Quartermaster Depot (BQD) which was responsible for the procurement of shoe items. Although the boots were reserved for the paratroopers, some of the Glider-borne troops wore them in combat, because of the esprit de corps, because they were 'Airborne' too.

Description

The new boots were mid-calf-length and made of the regulation russet colored leather. They had 12 pairs of eyelets (certain makes had eleven or thirteen pairs). The inside tongue had a gusset placed behind the laces and was sewn up to the top. This was reinforced with an overstitched backstay. The toe cap was very tough and had a pronounced bulge which gave the boot tip a distinctive 'bean' shape. The uppers were reinforced for ankle support by a strip of strong canvas sewn on the inside of the shoe revealing two, three or even four diagonal rows of stitching.

The Parachute Jumper Boots were laced up, without knots, to the top of the shaft. The M3 fighting knife is strapped to the leg and the bottom part of the M8 plastic sheath has been slipped into the boot. The two crossed rifles, pinned to the shirt collar indicate an infantry officer. He carries a Thompson SMG instead of the carbine normally issued to Platoon leaders.
(Reconstruction)

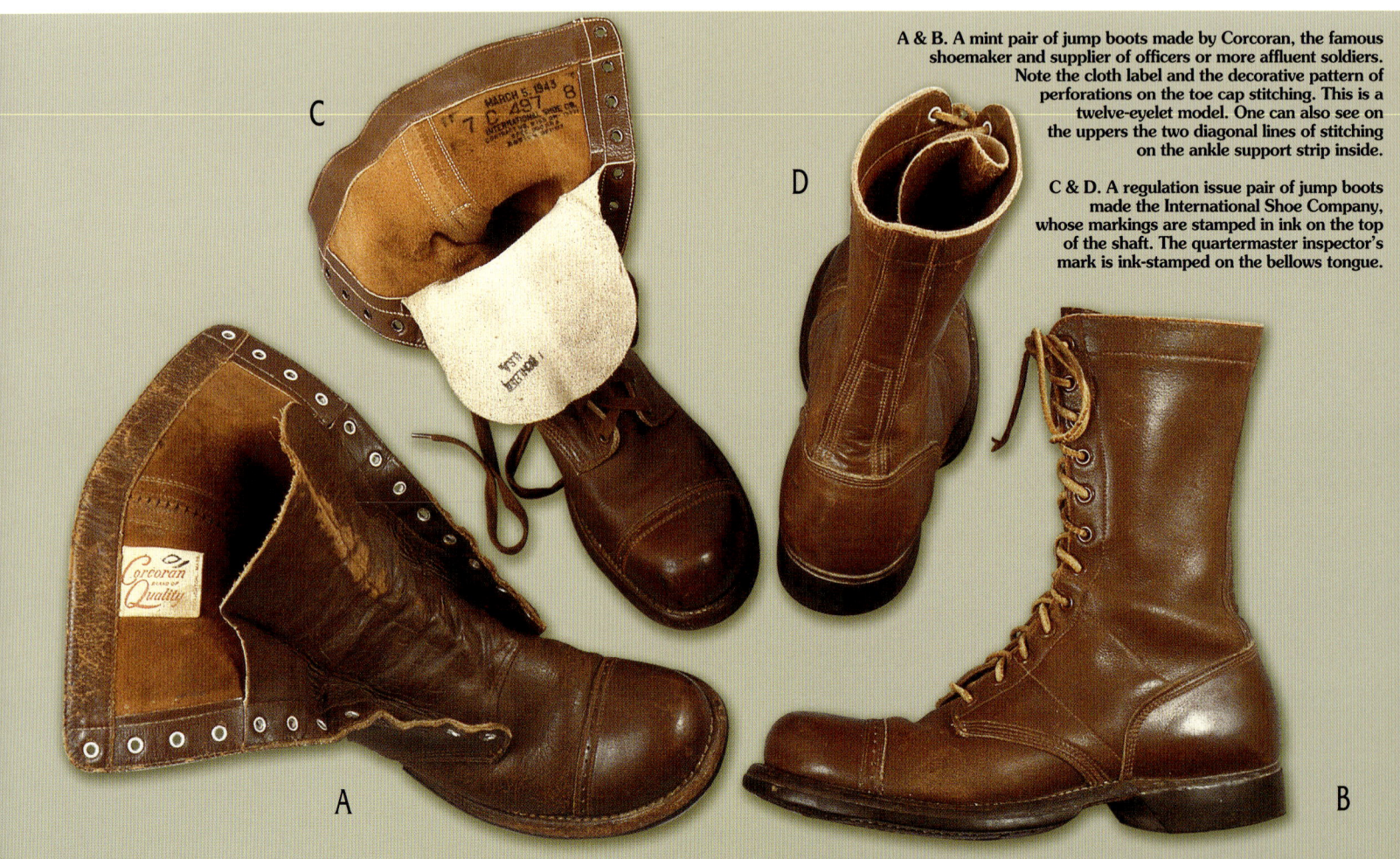

A & B. A mint pair of jump boots made by Corcoran, the famous shoemaker and supplier of officers or more affluent soldiers. Note the cloth label and the decorative pattern of perforations on the toe cap stitching. This is a twelve-eyelet model. One can also see on the uppers the two diagonal lines of stitching on the ankle support strip inside.

C & D. A regulation issue pair of jump boots made the International Shoe Company, whose markings are stamped in ink on the top of the shaft. The quartermaster inspector's mark is ink-stamped on the bellows tongue.

A good example of the influence of military technology on the civilian market: this advertisement uses the prestige associated with paratrooper boots to enhance Roblee, the civilian range of the Brown Shoe Co. The text in particular shows the protective qualities of the boots with reinforced toe and ankles as well as the beveled heels and the edge of the soles rounded to prevent the paratrooper from tripping during the jump.
(Author's collection)

The tap was made of black rubber with an anti-slip tread pattern, held by double stitching and brass tacks. The heel was made of the same rubber and had small alveoli round the edge which created the same effect as a shock absorber. It had a beveled front edge so parachute canopy shroud lines would not get entangled during the jump. The laces were made of brown cotton or natural leather.

The Quartermaster's catalogue for 1943 states that the 'Boots, parachute jumper' were available in 119 different sizes (Stock No 72-B-217 to 72-B-336-20)

Markings

The size was stamped on the outer leather sole just in front of the heel. It was also on the inside of the shaft, together with the maker's name, date and contract references, stamped in black ink or engraved on the leather.

The paratroopers were profoundly attached to their boots which, although meant for combat gear, were worn with off-duty and dress uniforms. The bottom of the trousers were neatly 'bloused' into the tops, revealing the boots, and distinguishing the paratroopers from the lowly 'leg' soldiers, who still had to contend with outmoded service shoes and laced canvas leggings.

A detailed look at the soles, with the beveled heel and the anti-slip tread pattern on the tap. The size is stamped on the sole, 7C for the right-hand pair and 8D for the Corcoran boots which have a distinctive 'C' on the heel. The heel and taps often bore the trademark of the largest US rubber companies.
(Photo Militaria Magazine)

49

CHAPTER 5 THE PARATROOPER HELMET

M2 Steel Helmet

When the airborne troops were created in 1941, the new M1 Helmet which had recently been approved by the US Army was in fact not adapted to the parachute jump: the shell and liner were separate, the chinstrap was uncomfortable and the helmet was not very steady on the wearer's head. Rather than create a special helmet, the Army tried to adapt the standard issue. On the helmet shell, the rectangular chinstrap loops were replaced by curved loops which facilitated the chinstrap's sideways movement.

The chinstraps were lengthened and fitted on each side with a short tab provided with a male press stud which fastened into the female part riveted inside the liner, thus holding the two helmet components together. The helmet was given the designation 'M2' and standardized by the QMC on 23 June 1942. 148,000 shells with paratrooper chinstraps were produced by the Mac Cord Company between January 1942 and December 1944.

On the liner, special inverted A-shaped straps were added on each side. Each was fitted with a buckle which received a leather chamois-lined chin cup. The helmet thus modified was much more stable on the wearer's head.

The first paratrooper liners were modified early type, canvas-covered fibre liners. They had a distinguishing rounded edge around the rim. These early liners were produced by Hawley and modified into the paratrooper version by Mac Cord Radiator. But the fibre liners turned out to be too fragile: they were easily dented and were not resistant to humidity. They were adequately replaced by the new plastic liners (resin-covered canvas, heat and pressure-shaped in a mold), which were more resilient. The first production run of paratrooper plastic liners was carried out by Inland Manufacturing, a division of General Motors, the paratrooper modification being undertaken by Mac Cord Radiator; the second batch was made by Westinghouse. About 148,000 were produced.

Towards the Helmet, Steel, Parachutist M1C

In October 1943, the QMC decided to modify the loops for the chinstrap on the M1 Helmet shell. Instead of being fixed, they were hinged. The paratrooper-style chinstraps were also fitted to this new shell. Although production of the new shell started at the end of 1943, it did not appear in the QMC catalogue under the designation 'Parachutist Helmet M1C' until January 1945. It does not seem to have been used in Normandy.

A study of period photographs and the few helmet relics found on the battlefield reveals quite a few points: some of the paratroopers still had the early fibre liner, and many M2 helmets feature broken and re-soldered rings, some of them actually replaced by substitute metal fittings (field bag rings, etc.). These helmets had no doubt been repaired by workshops in England. A few M1 helmet shells (with square fixed chinstrap loops) seem to have been factory-made with paratrooper chinstraps. This was probably a stop-gap measure after the M2 production had stopped and before the M1C production had begun. The one and only example we could study had nickel-plated studs on the chinstrap tabs, just like the M2.

Paratroopers were also commonly issued with standard M1 shells (with the regular chinstrap) mated to a paratrooper-type liner.

Painting - Camouflage - Insignia

All M1/M2 helmet shells were factory-painted in light olive drab paint mixed with particles of cork, which gave them their grained matt look. This reduced glare and noise, if the helmet hit something. With use, the finish got smoother and shinier; the color changed to brown. Many helmets found in Normandy show that they had been repainted with a brush before D-Day because of the wear and tear of the numerous training operations in the spring of 1944 in England. A majority of paratroopers covered their helmets with British- or Canadian-made camouflage netting, in different mesh sizes. Very often brown jute cloth strips were knotted into the net, noticeably improving the camouflage. More rarely, the camouflage of the helmets was painted: wide dark sand, green or black stripes were applied. Dull yellow gas detection paint was sometimes used. Some of these camouflage schemes dated back to operations in Sicily.

Rank markings were generally painted on the front for the officers, more rarely for the NCOs (sometimes on the side). To make officers easier to identify by the soldiers, a vertical white stripe was painted on the rear of the helmet for the officers (horizontally for the NCOs).

Arm-of-service symbols were also painted on the helmets: initials for MPs, crosses for medical personnel and chaplains, etc.

Within the 101st Airborne Division was a whole system of tactical signs painted on helmets. This resulted from a staff conference held two weeks before D-Day. In this as yet untried division, the command was seeking a method with which to identify the men and their units as soon as they reached the ground. The suggestion was to paint easy-to-remember signs on the helmets: the four aces from a pack of cards, as well as

(Continued on page 56)

Paratrooper M2 Helmet with its leather chin cup. The rounded chinstrap loops are clearly visible.

Close-up of the M2 Helmet opposite. Note the granite paint finish and the factory-stitched chinstrap. The D-Ring sticks out from under the rim of the helmet (the reason for so many breakages).
In the background, note the square buckles of the Inland liner, made of chemically-blackened steel.

THE M2 HELMET

Left and below.
Close-up of the chinstraps of an M2 helmet. Note the square tips of the D-ring, welded onto the shell, and the nickel-plated press studs on the chinstrap tabs, typical of the M2 Helmet.

A paratrooper liner made by Inland. Note the tan color (Shade No 3) of the chin cup webbing straps.

(Private collection)

51

THE M2 HELMET
(SAINT-CLAIR LINER)

Brass chin cup buckle mounted on the Saint-Clair liner.

This M2 Helmet found at Neuville au Plain belonged to Staff-Sergeant Thomas R. Vaughn of the 507th PIR (82nd Airborne), killed on 7 June 1944. The shell chinstrap had been damaged and repaired at the time with a rivet.

Paratrooper liner produced by the Saint Clair Rubber Company: it could be distinguished from the other makes by its slightly indented rim where the shell D-rings were situated, by the smooth and glossy paintwork, and finally. The early thin leather chinstrap is riveted inside the liner.

Inside view of the Saint-Clair liner. The inside is painted olive green. All lining straps are the gray rayon of early plastic liners. The snap-on headband was not adjustable and there were several sizes. Only the front part was covered with leather.

(Private collection)

PARATROOPER HELMET LINERS

Close-up of the squarish chin cup buckle of an Inland Liner. It is made of copper-plated steel, that has blackened with age.

How the straps were fixed on the paratrooper conversion of the Inland liner. Note the nickel-plated female press stud on the inside of the helmet.

A Westinghouse liner. Note the olive green color of the webbing (Shade No 7) which appeared towards the end of 1943.

Close-up of the buckles and inverted A straps of a Westinghouse liner. Note the rounded shape of the olive-green painted cast alloy chin cup buckles.

(Private collection)

Three types of leather chin cups used on paratrooper liners.

Repaired D-rings on an M2 helmet.

Opposite.
This striking propaganda photograph was taken in the United States in August 1943. The man in the foreground has one of the early T-5 parachutes, with white harness and unpainted buckles. It does not have either the ring for the weapon padded case, at shoulder level on the right. The rounded chinstrap loop of the M2 helmet shell can be clearly seen here.
This parachutist's equipment has been reduced to a minimum: note the pouch for the compass partly hidden by the parachute chest pack.
(National Archives)

THE M2 HELMET

M1 Helmet shell with fixed square ring, fitted with a paratrooper chinstrap.
Note the nickel-plated pressure stud on the chinstrap tab, just like on the M2.

This M2 helmet from the 3/501st PIR (101st Airborne div.) still has its original netting. The regimental markings have been covered with a thin coat of paint (probably gas detection paint) to make them less visible.
(Musée de la Seconde Guerre Mondiale, Ambleteuse)

Private collection except otherwise mentioned

54

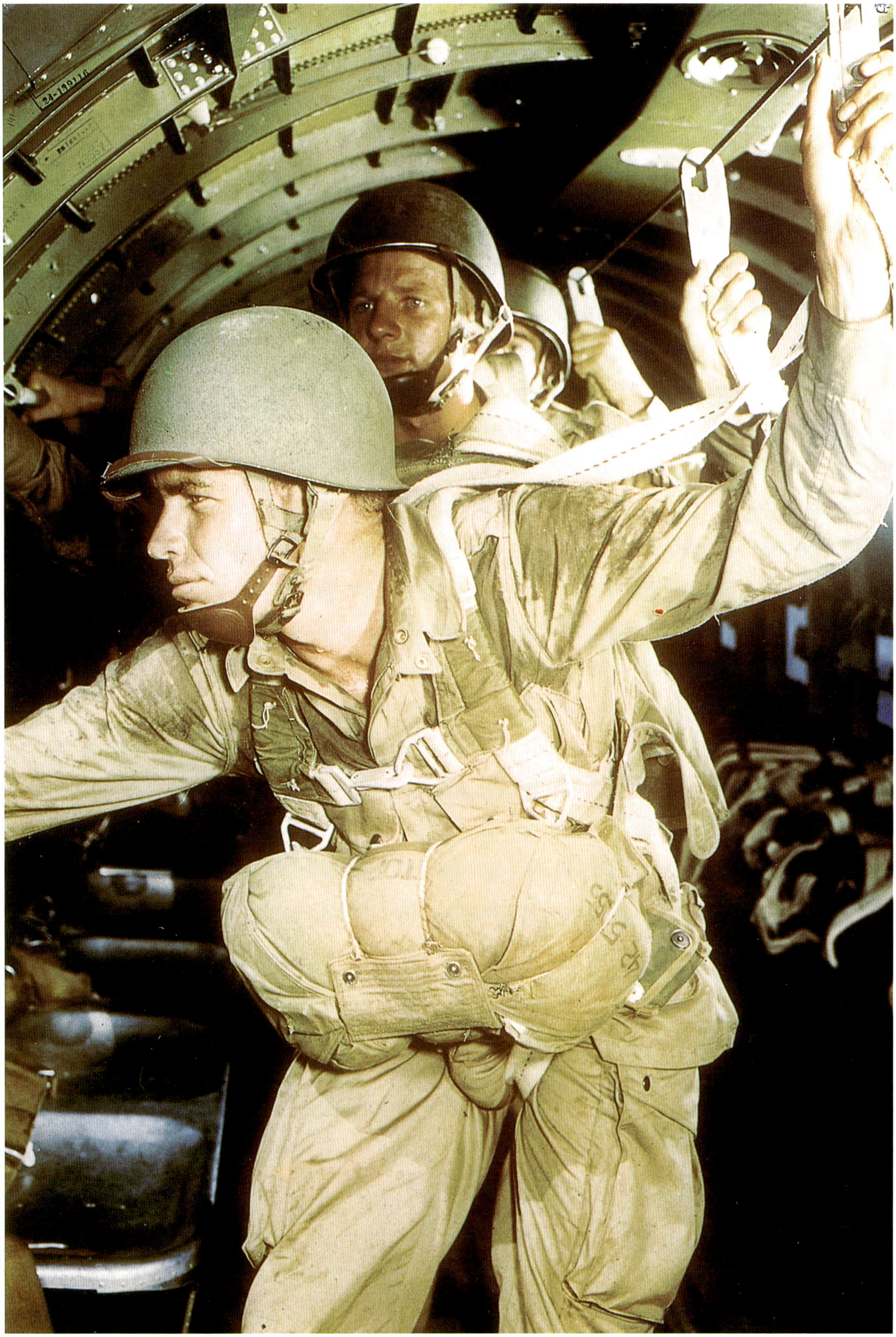

101st AIRBORNE DIVISION HELMET MARKINGS

♣ 327th Field Inf. Regt	♦ 501st PIR	♥ 502d PIR	♠ 506th PIR
321st Glider Field Artillery Battalion	377th Parachute Field Artillery Battalion	907th Glider Field Artillery Battalion	463d Parachute Field Artillery Battalion
HQ Divisional Artillery	81st AAA Battalion	101st Reconnaissance Platoon	326th Engineer Battalion
101st Signal Co	426th QM Company	801st Ordnance Company	326th Medical Company

82nd AIRBORNE DIVISION

- HQ Co/508th PIR (red letters HH)
- ?/507 PIR (white diabolo)
- 3/508th PIR (winged foot)

Headquarters / 3nd Battalion / 1st Battalion / 2nd Battalion

The position of the white dash indicated:
- on top: Unit HQ
- on the right: 1st battalion
- underneath: 2nd battalion
- on the left: 3rd battalion

(Continued from page 50)

simple geometrical shapes (see page 56). Endorsed by General Maxwell D. Taylor, the division commander, the plan was immediately put into practice. These insignia were about 1 3/4 high and painted in white on either side of the helmet. It was thanks to the account given by Major-General G.J. Higgins, Chief-of-Staff of the 101st in 1944 that the meaning of these markings was revealed.

The 82nd Airborne's helmets on the other hand were on the whole more sober, we note:

– A winged foot painted on the helmets of the 3rd Battalion of the 508th P.I.R., commanded by Lieutenant-Colonel Louis Mendez,
- The red letters HH on the helmets of the HQs and HQ Company of the 508th.
- A small white diabolo painted on the helmets of one battalion of the 507th PIR.

An M2 helmet belonging to Captain Charles O. Van Gorder of the 326th Airborne Medical Company of the 101st Airborne Division. Van Gorder certified the death of General Pratt killed in his glider on landing, on 6 June 1944.

A helmet found at Catz having belonged to Leo C. German (army serial number 36475316), B Co. 506th PIR, 101st Airborne div., killed in June 1944. The motif painted on the front is unusual: a wolf howling at the moon. The helmet shell is a standard M1.

This helmet belonged to a NCO of the 501 PIR (101 A/B), found near Mont Castre. A bullet pierced it.

An 82nd Airborne NCO's helmet, found at Méautis.

(Private collection)

An M2 Helmet for a 307th AB Medical Co. NCO (82nd A/B div).
The broken D-rings have been replaced by home-made rectangular loops.

Paratrooper liner made by Westinghouse, markings for a medic in the 82nd Airborne division.

Paratrooper liner made by Westinghouse, found at Auvers. Markings for a Military Policeman.

Camouflaged paratrooper helmet, 82nd Airborne division. On the front is a decal of the paratrooper wings. The helmet shell is a standard M1 fitted with an Inland paratrooper liner.

(Private collection)

Paratrooper helmet from the 1st Platoon of C Company, 326th Airborne Engineer Battalion (101st A/B div.). The helmet shell is a standard M1 equipped with paratrooper chinstraps (the tabs with press studs got in the way after landing and have been cut off) combined with an Inland para liner.

Helmet from the 3rd Battalion, 506th Regiment, 101st A/B div. belonging to Technician 5th Grade William H. Atlee, killed at Saint-Côme-du-Mont on 6 June 1944 and whose body lies in the cemetery at Saint-Laurent-sur-Mer. Unusually, the dot designating the battalion has been painted on the wrong side of the ace of spades (designating the 1/506). In order to be able to identify each other the paratroopers added the dot on the front and the rear of the helmet.

Helmet from the 502nd PIR of the 101st Airborne. The ace of hearts, here the smaller variant, more likely represents later operations (Market-Garden). The helmet shell is the standard M1 mated to a Westinghouse liner.

Standard M1 Helmet shell bearing the markings of the 2nd Battalion of the 327th Glider Infantry Regiment.

(Private collection)

59

Sergeant Corrington's Inland-made liner, bearing his name and number. He also penciled on the top:
'Left America by sea 13 November 1943, landed England 3 December 43.'

M2 Helmet found at Basse-Addeville belonging to Sergeant Floyd J. Corrington, army service number 19127607, from D Company (2nd Battalion) of the 506th PIR/101st Airborne div., killed on 6 June 1944 at Addeville. The horizontal stripe indicates an NCO; note the dull yellow gas detection paint splotches.

M2 helmet shell holed by a shell burst found in the marshes at Saint-Martin de Varreville.

Vesicant Gas Detector Paint, here the British issue

(Private collection)

M2 helmet belonging to a paratrooper NCO from Item Company of the 505th PIR, 82nd Airborne.

Top.
Tiredness shows on the face of this paratrooper from the 82nd airborne division. His M2 helmet is covered by British-issue fine-mesh netting.
(Reconstruction)

Camouflaged helmet from the 82nd Airborne division fitted with a Westinghouse liner.

(Private collection)

CHAPTER 6: THE T-5 PARACHUTE

The T-5 parachute appeared in 1941, as a result of joint studies made by the Army Air Corps and the Fort Benning Infantry School (Georgia). Trials were held from July 1940 by the Parachute Test Platoon, made up of volunteers from the 29th Infantry Regiment.

Although it was modern for the period, the T-5 parachute had one important flaw: its harness buckles locking system. Indeed if a paratrooper who was to land under fire or in a flooded area, it was vital once on the ground to be able to release himself from his chute as quickly as possible. On the T-5 there were at least three snap hooks to be released, one on the breastbone and two between the legs. To cap it all, these hooks were difficult to get at when the paratrooper was wearing all his combat equipment. This serious defect cost the lives of countless US paratroopers, drowned in the marshes of the Merderet, tangled up in their harness. The only emergency solution was to cut the harness open with a knife, and proof is the large numbers of cut-up T-5 harnesses recovered from the battlefield.

Where the chest pack was concerned, this was considered as a luxury by the English and Germans who had to trust the main pack alone. And it was not of much use on 6 June 1944, since most of the jumps took place from an average altitude of 500 feet which allowed just enough time for the main chute to open and slow the paratrooper down before he hit the ground.

The T-5 Parachute

The following descriptions refer mainly to the color plate on page 63 showing the T-5 parachute harness, and also to the photographs on pages 66-67.

At dusk on 5 June at Upottery Base. These Screaming Eagles are putting the final touch to their gear. This excellent picture shows the great variety in the issue and method of positioning equipment for the jump.
The paratrooper on the left is carrying his E-tool on his right hip and has a padded sheath for his weapon. His comrade on the other hand has hung his shovel on the left-hand side and is carrying his M1 rifle vertically under the arm, hanging from its sling. The sub-machine gun magazine bag probably contains ammunition. The M5 Gas Mask is clearly visible under the Main chute pack. Also note the way the belly band has been threaded into its buckle, maybe a kind of makeshift quick-release device.
(National Archives)

The Canopy

This was made of nylon with a camouflage pattern of small green and brown spots. It had a surface area of 566 sq. ft. and was made up of 28 gores. In the center, there was a 1 ft 5 in opening - the chimney - to let the air escape and give better stability during the descent. There were twenty-eight 22 foot-long shroud lines spread round the circumference and linking the shroud to the elevators on the harness (g & h, opposite page).

The Harness

This was made up of a set of webbing straps, white on the early models then olive drab. They were fastened on the chest by means of a snap hook (1) placed on the right strap of the main harness which then fastened to a ring (2) situated on the left-hand strap. The four straps formed a flat Vee at the harness bottom, thus forming a kind of seat (3) on which the paratrooper rested. From this seat, there were two adjustable thigh straps (4 & 5) which went between the paratrooper's legs to fasten onto the front of the harness (6 & 7). The chest pack hooks were attached to the two D-shaped rings (8 & 9) on the front harness straps.

A V-shaped ring sewn at shoulder level (10) received the snap hook for the padded holster of the M1 rifle or any other bag/case.

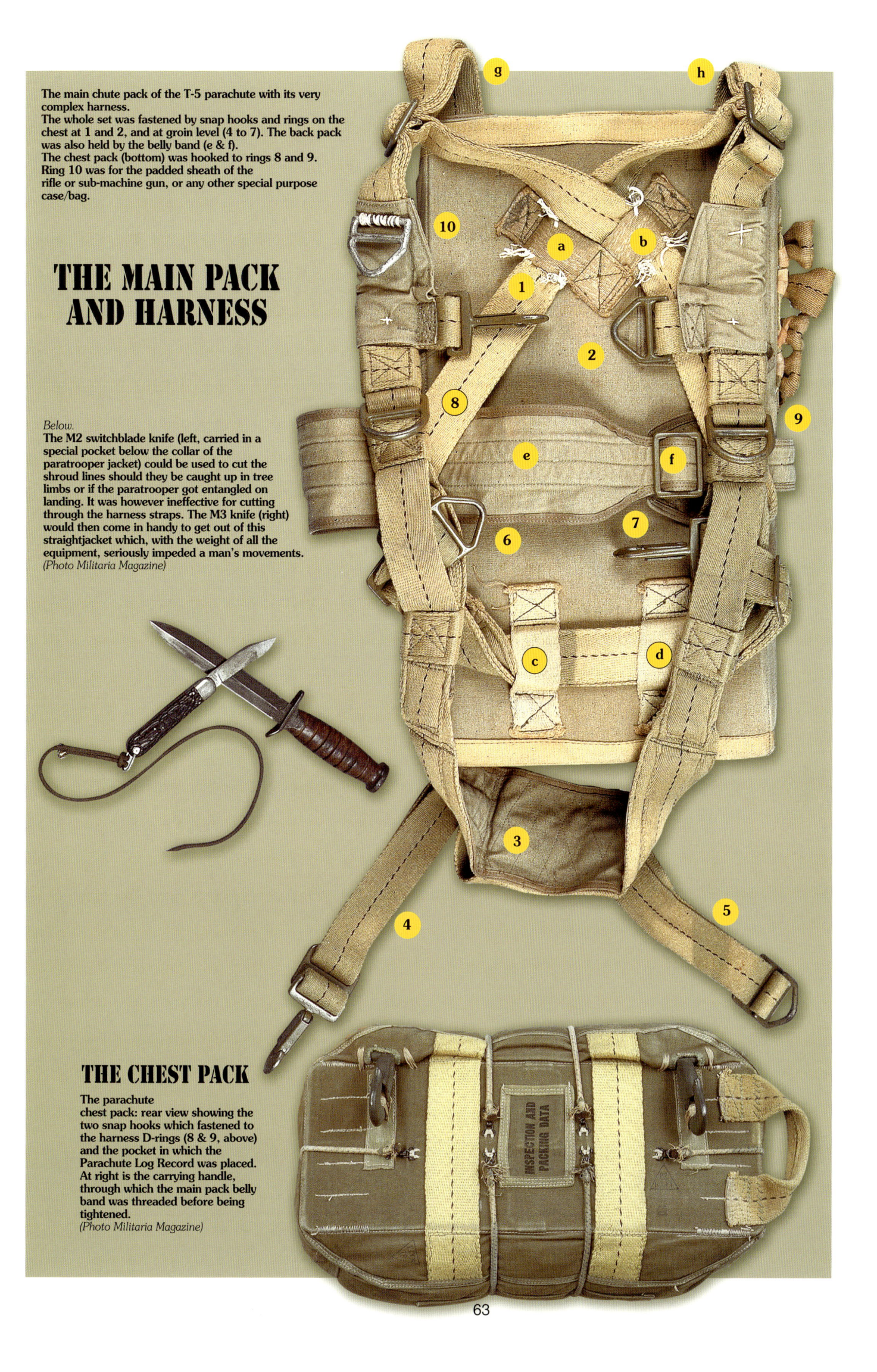

The main chute pack of the T-5 parachute with its very complex harness.
The whole set was fastened by snap hooks and rings on the chest at 1 and 2, and at groin level (4 to 7). The back pack was also held by the belly band (e & f).
The chest pack (bottom) was hooked to rings 8 and 9. Ring 10 was for the padded sheath of the rifle or sub-machine gun, or any other special purpose case/bag.

THE MAIN PACK AND HARNESS

Below.
The M2 switchblade knife (left, carried in a special pocket below the collar of the paratrooper jacket) could be used to cut the shroud lines should they be caught up in tree limbs or if the paratrooper got entangled on landing. It was however ineffective for cutting through the harness straps. **The M3 knife** (right) would then come in handy to get out of this straightjacket which, with the weight of all the equipment, seriously impeded a man's movements.
(Photo Militaria Magazine)

THE CHEST PACK

The parachute chest pack: rear view showing the two snap hooks which fastened to the harness D-rings (8 & 9, above) and the pocket in which the Parachute Log Record was placed. At right is the carrying handle, through which the main pack belly band was threaded before being tightened.
(Photo Militaria Magazine)

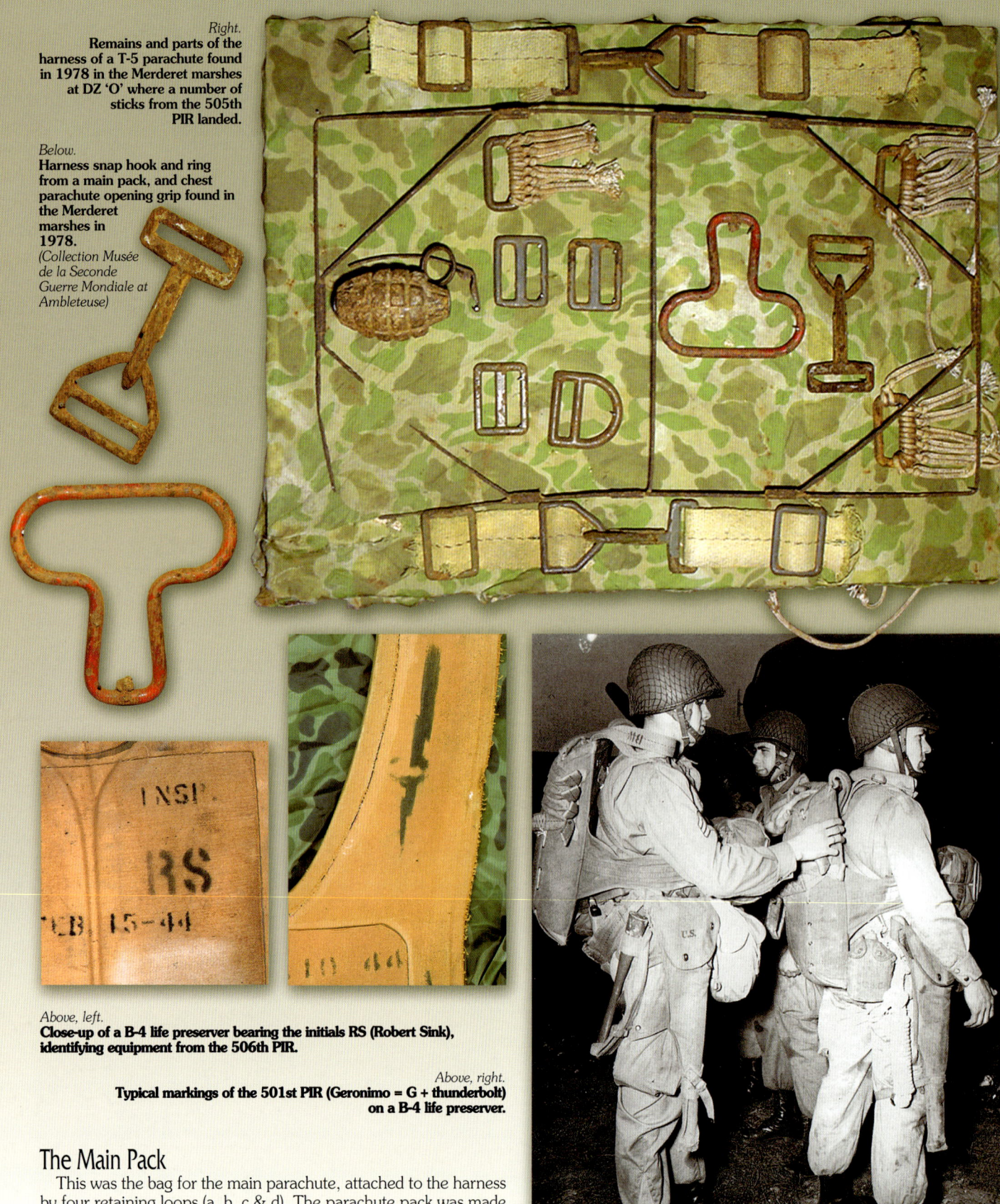

Right.
Remains and parts of the harness of a T-5 parachute found in 1978 in the Merderet marshes at DZ 'O' where a number of sticks from the 505th PIR landed.

Below.
Harness snap hook and ring from a main pack, and chest parachute opening grip found in the Merderet marshes in 1978.
(Collection Musée de la Seconde Guerre Mondiale at Ambleteuse)

Above, left.
Close-up of a B-4 life preserver bearing the initials RS (Robert Sink), identifying equipment from the 506th PIR.

Above, right.
Typical markings of the 501st PIR (Geronimo = G + thunderbolt) on a B-4 life preserver.

The Main Pack

This was the bag for the main parachute, attached to the harness by four retaining loops (a, b, c & d). The parachute pack was made rigid by a metal framed back pad which rested on the soldier's back. This pad had four wide flaps which made up and closed the sides of the pack. There were 24 eyelets round the four flaps. On the pad vertical edges were sewn two wide belly bands (e & f); the one on the right measured 2 ft 11 in and the one on the left 6 in., ending with a strong square buckle. The belly band was tightened on the front after slipping through the chest pack handle (page 64, bottom), thus joining the back and chest packs. On the outside of the main pack, there was a small pocket (there was a similar one on the chest pack), marked 'Inspection and Packing Data' and which contained the Parachute Log Record.

When the parachute had been packed, a piece of rectangular cloth,

These parachute artillerymen are checking their main packs before boarding for a training jump a short time before D-Day. The sergeant on the left is carrying the M-1910 pick mattock on his belt and an M1A1 Carbine in its sheath. Clearly visible on the static line are the initials BW showing that this NCO belongs to the 377th PFABn, commanded by Lt. Col. Benjamin Weisberg.
(National Archives)

Left.
The following are set out on a T-5 Parachute canopy as a backdrop:
- Parachute Log Record indicating the number and dates of jumps together with repairs and overhauls. From the open copy, the last training jump was made in Britain on 21 April 1944.
- Phosphorescent Marker fastened on the paratrooper's back, or on some other item of equipment enabling the man behind to follow on. It was also used to locate parachuted equipment on the ground.
- Escape compass (see page 96).
(Photo Militaria Magazine)

Below.
A paratrooper is being helped with his parachute harness. He has the folding carbine in the special holster slipped on the belt. The deflated life preserver is another hindrance. In case of a 'wet' landing, the paratrooper must unhook the chest pack before trying to inflate his 'Mae West,' a very difficult task in an emergency. The M-1936 musette bag has been placed back to front at groin level, an additional garment (raincoat?) is folded under its flap.
(National Archives)

the 'cover' closed the main chute bag by means of a cotton cord called the 'breaking string.'

The Static Line

This was a 15-foot long strap which was neatly folded and held on the main chute pack thanks to elastic bands attached to retaining loops sewn onto its flaps. One end of the Static line was attached to the 'cover' by means of a very strong harness strap loop which was tied to the parachute's chimney (by means of another 'breaking string'). The other end bore a large snap hook which the paratrooper attached to the cable running along the ceiling of the aircraft cabin. When the paratrooper jumped out of the plane, the static line was brutally unwound and tightened; it separated from the elastic bands which held it onto the back pack and when fully unraveled, the 'cover' was ripped out, breaking the string and pulling the canopy out. After the shroud had 'blossomed,' the static line and cover remained attached and floated in the slipstream.

The chest pack

Its canopy was made of nylon with a surface area of 490 sq. ft. The pack was made up of a rigid rectangle and four flaps. In an emergency, it was manually opened by pulling on an aluminium or steel handle, often painted red. The envelope opened immediately thanks to six elastic cords pulled tight over the flaps.

On the back of the pack, two snap hooks were attached to the strong D-rings of the main harness (8 & 9). The main pack's belly band was also threaded through the chest pack carrying handle.

Special markings on jump equipment

Equipment found in the field has revealed stencil marks which were specific to the 101st Airborne. They are to be found on the parachute harness, the chest packs (on the rear), B-4 life preservers and weapons' padded ('Griswold') bags.

Examples of markings (see page 64):
- The initial G struck by a black lightning flash = 501st PIR
- Initials GVM for George Van H. Moseley, the 502nd PIR CO
- RS for Robert Sink, the 506th PIR CO
- BW for Benjamin Weisberg, the 377th PFABn. CO

The object of these regimental marks was to discourage 'tactless borrowing' between units.

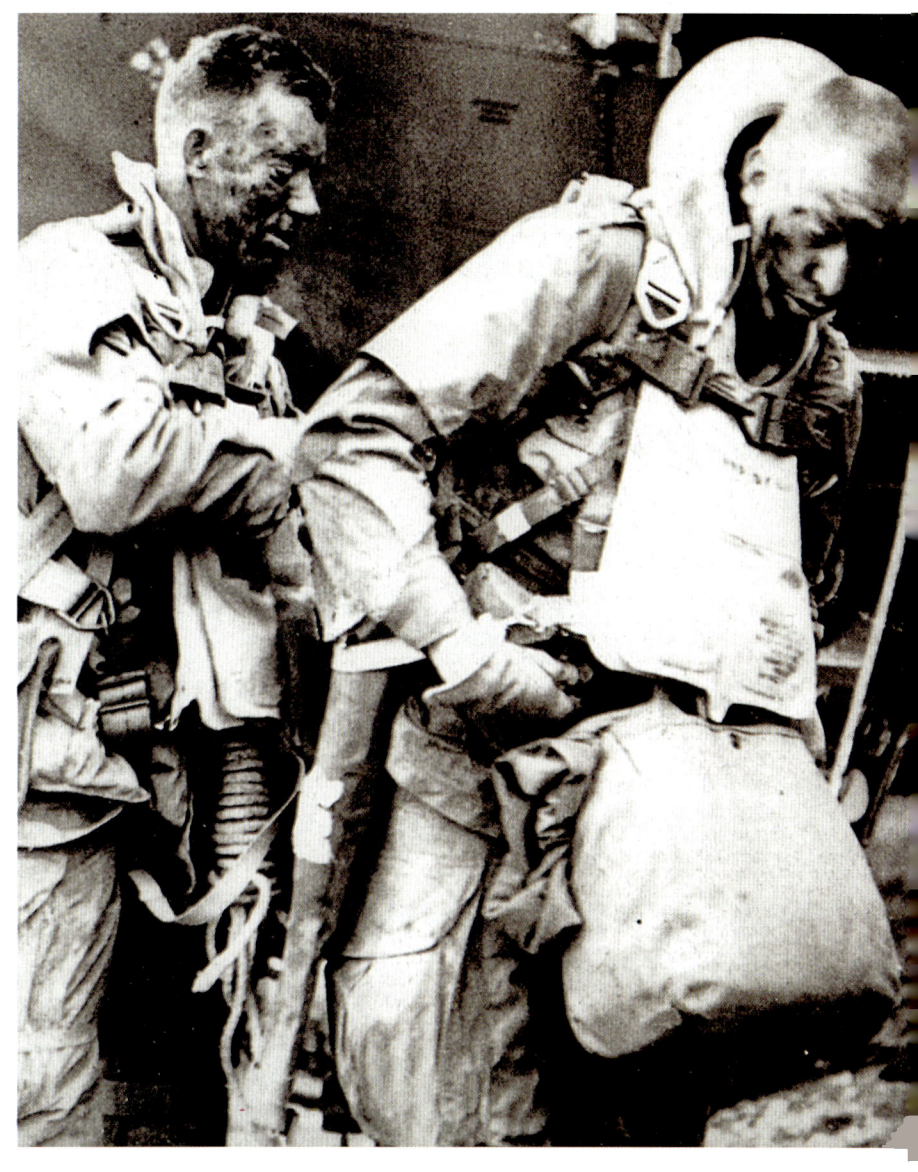

1- The Static Line went over the arm (not under the arm, or the paratrooper would be in for a surprise when the chute opened). The M-1943 shovel was used concurrently with the M-1910 which was more dangerous when jumping because of its T-shaped handle. The gas mask was placed in its waterproof rubber bag, one strap round the waist the other around the leg. A British Hawkins anti-tank mine has been tied to the calf for the jump, in the same way as the Paratrooper First Aid Packet to the jump boot.

2- The parachute harness was buckled over the life-preserver, which prevented its inflating in an emergency. The M-1936 musette bag was placed back to front below the chest pack, hooked by its staps to the pistol belt. Its flap buckles were thus out of the way of the shroud lines.
(Reconstruction)

Note. The jump suit shown here belonged to a paratrooper of the 82nd A/B division who was wounded during a training jump in England just before D-Day. The T-5 parachute (without the Cover) was offered to a stuntman in the film, 'the Longest Day' by an inhabitant of Sainte-Mère-Eglise who put him up while the film was being shot.

3- On this rear view, the green canvas reinforcing on the jacket's elbows and the trousers cargo pockets bellows can be clearly seen. Note also the straps which compressed these pockets.

4- Ammunition for the Thompson SMG is carried in a British-made magazine bag. The carefully coiled 'rope parachutist's' was very useful if he landed in trees or on a roof; the M3 fighting knife, in its M8 plastic scabbard is fastened to the calf by a strap taken from a salvaged haversack. The Thompson sub-machine gun, without a special padded jump case, has been slung over the paratrooper's shoulder and stuck under the parachute pack belly band. The Thompson SMG was not part of the parachute infantry squad TO&E, it was carried by some HQ Co. personnel and soldiers who preferred it to the rifle or carbine at close quarters
(Reconstruction)

1. T-5 Parachute chest pack, version for airborne troops.

2. AN 6513-1A parachute chest pack, exactly the same as the previous one but with the United States Army Air Forces (USAAF) nomenclature.

3. Rear view of a T-5 chest pack. Note the initials RS (Robert Sink) identifying it as a piece of equipment belonging to the 506th PIR (101st Airborne Division).

4. Rear view of a T-5 chest pack AN 6513-1A with the initials GVM of George Van H. Moseley, the 502nd PIR CO.

5. Rear view of a T-5 chest pack with the initials BW of Lt.-Col. Benjamin Weisberg, the 377th PFABn CO.

6. T-5 Parachute harness found at Sainte-Mère-Eglise twenty years ago.
(Private Collection except where specified)

(Yann Le Vu collection)

6 June in the morning: under the watchful eye of a Staff Sergeant (on the left), these glider troops from the 82d Division are getting ready for the last weapons and equipment check before they leave to reinforce the bridgehead. The men have been issued with yellow rubberized canvas lifejackets, and M4 lightweight gas masks in their oblong canvas bags.
The gliders, British Airspeed Horsas have been only recently delivered to the American Army since the RAF roundels have not been entirely repainted.
(National Archives)

CHAPTER 7 THE GLIDER-BORNE TROOPS

NICKNAMED 'Glider Riders' by their paratrooper comrades, the Glider troops were considered as the poor relations of the Airborne divisions. They nevertheless fought very creditably, given the haphazard way they joined the battle.

Paratroopers were all volunteers and received a bonus of $50 for each combat jump whereas the glider troops, who were regular table of organization units, could only expect the likelihood of taking a tumble in their glider when it crashed on one of 'Rommel's asparagus' or the high clumps of devilish Norman hedgerows…

Their training on the ground was just as intensive as that of the paratroopers but their uniforms and equipment were identical to those of other 'leg' soldiers. Only the divisional patch distinguished glider troops from the regular infantry division units.

As to glider pilots, some them realized with horror shortly before take-off, that the second pilot sitting next to them was an Army private with vague notions of flying and who had never even landed or taken off in a glider.

Cartoon drawn by Dale Oliver, a Waco glider pilot who took part in Operation Neptune (7 June).
(DR)

69

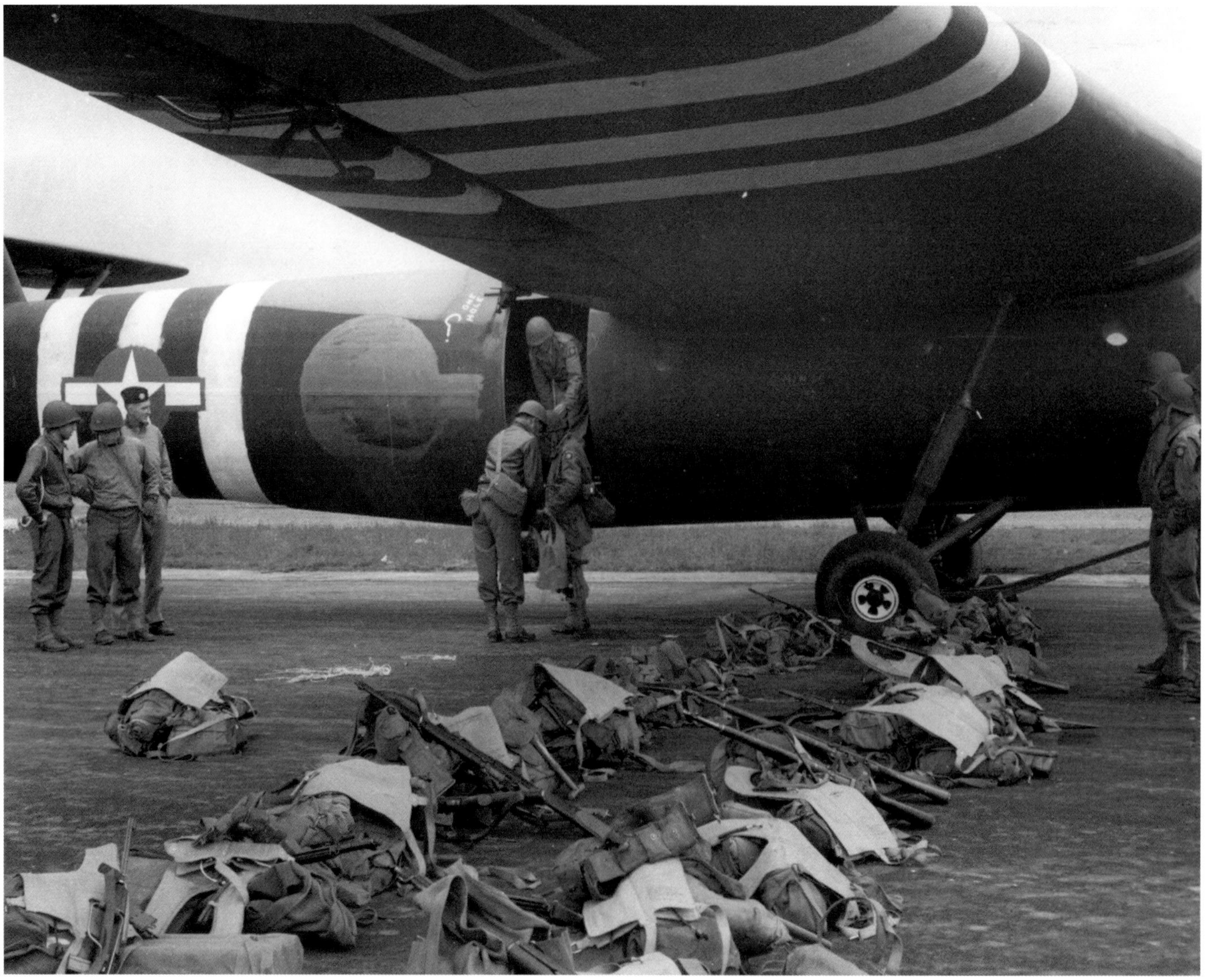

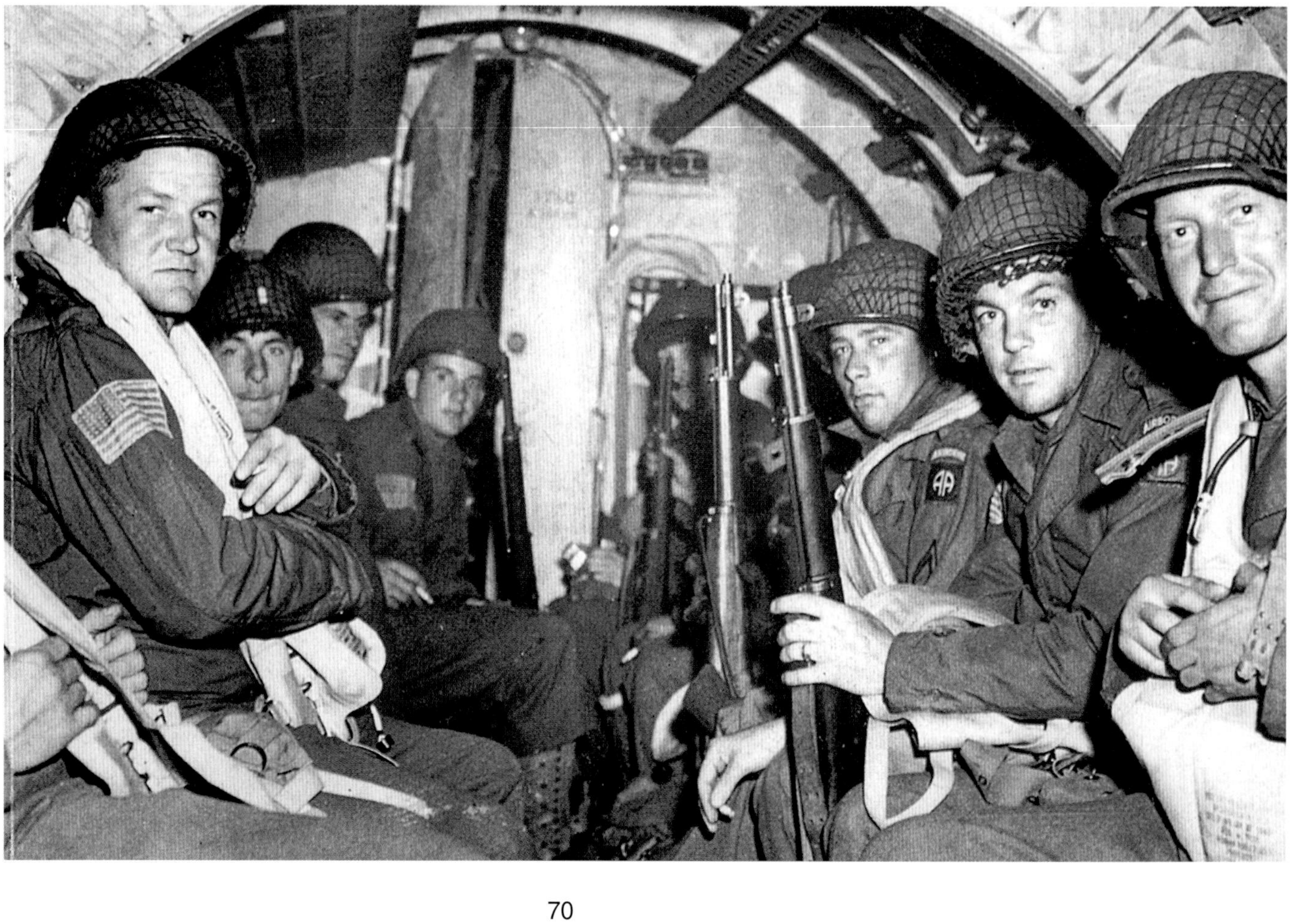

Previous page, top.
Before boarding, these glider troops from the 82nd A/B division have lined up their packs, life belts and weapons under the wing of a Horsa glider. The British roundel has hastily been covered over and the USAAF 'star and bar' marking painted further back.

Above.
These glider troops from the 82nd A/B division (identified by the nationality flags on the right sleeve) are heading for their gliders, preceded by men from the Military Police. Note that some of the latter have managed to get hold of jump boots, an item very much in demand and issued normally only to the paratroopers.

Previous page, bottom.
6 June 1944: this time it's no longer an exercise and these glider infantrymen, piled into a Horsa glider, show their anxiety, despite the smiles for the photographer… The glider tugs belong to the 439th Troop Carrier Group, for which this is the second mission over the Cotentin Peninsula: the previous evening they had embarked the men of the 101st A/B for the first drops. All the men are wearing the standard uniform: field jacket with the 82nd A/B sleeve patch and the flag, woolen trousers and M1 helmet. The soldier on the right has an early helmet liner, made of compressed fibre and covered in canvas.
(Photos National Archives)

71

Glider Troops Officer, 101st Airborne division

Apart from the patch of the 101st Airborne div. sewn on the left-hand sleeve, nothing distinguishes this officer from a regular infantry officer. His jump boots, non-regulation in Glider units, may well have been bought from the PX or from a paratrooper chum. The gas mask should normally have been the Amphibious Assault gas mask M5 reserved for assault units; however, upon examination of period documents it seems that not all units were systematically equipped with them.

The M3 fighting knife in its leather M6 sheath was regulation issue for personnel armed with carbines. The pistol holster, the waterproofed compass pouch, the knife and canteen are all attached to the belt. The pistol belt is held up by the M-1936 suspenders. The Parachute first aid packet (page 100) is tied to the left hand side set of straps, a smoke grenade is held by its spoon on the right hand side.
The officer also has binoculars in their leather case and a map case (slung under his right arm). The vesicant gas detection armband is worn on the right arm.
(Reconstruction, Militaria Magazine)

Below.
A glider pilot (right), a glider-borne infantryman of the 82nd A/B division (centre) and a paratrooper from the same division (left) talking to a paratroop officer from the 101st A/B (gas detection armband) who has been dropped far from his DZ.
(Reconstruction)

Above.
The wreck of this Horsa shows how hard the landings could often be! Even built with lightweight materials, this British-made glider could reach a weight of 7 tonnes when loaded. Speed, darkness, Rommel's asparaguses or 'these bloody hedges' all vouched for rough landings. Dozens of glider pilots and soldiers paid for this with their lives.
(National Archives)

73

The hinged nose of the CG-4A Waco glider made loading and unloading easy. The jeep trailer, loaded with stretchers, bears markings for the 325th GIR's medical detachment.
(National Archives)

USAAF Glider Pilot

Although they were part of the Air Force, glider pilots were outfitted just like other glider borne soldiers: M1 helmet, olive drab field jacket, wool trousers or the herringbone twill one-piece suit (as shown here), leggings and service shoes.
After landing, glider pilots would often find themselves in the midst of battle, so they were armed with the rifle, bayonet and grenades. These valuable trained personnel were however ordered to make it back to Allied lines as soon as possible for shipment to England.
(Another glider pilot silhouette is illustrated on page 24)
(Reconstruction)

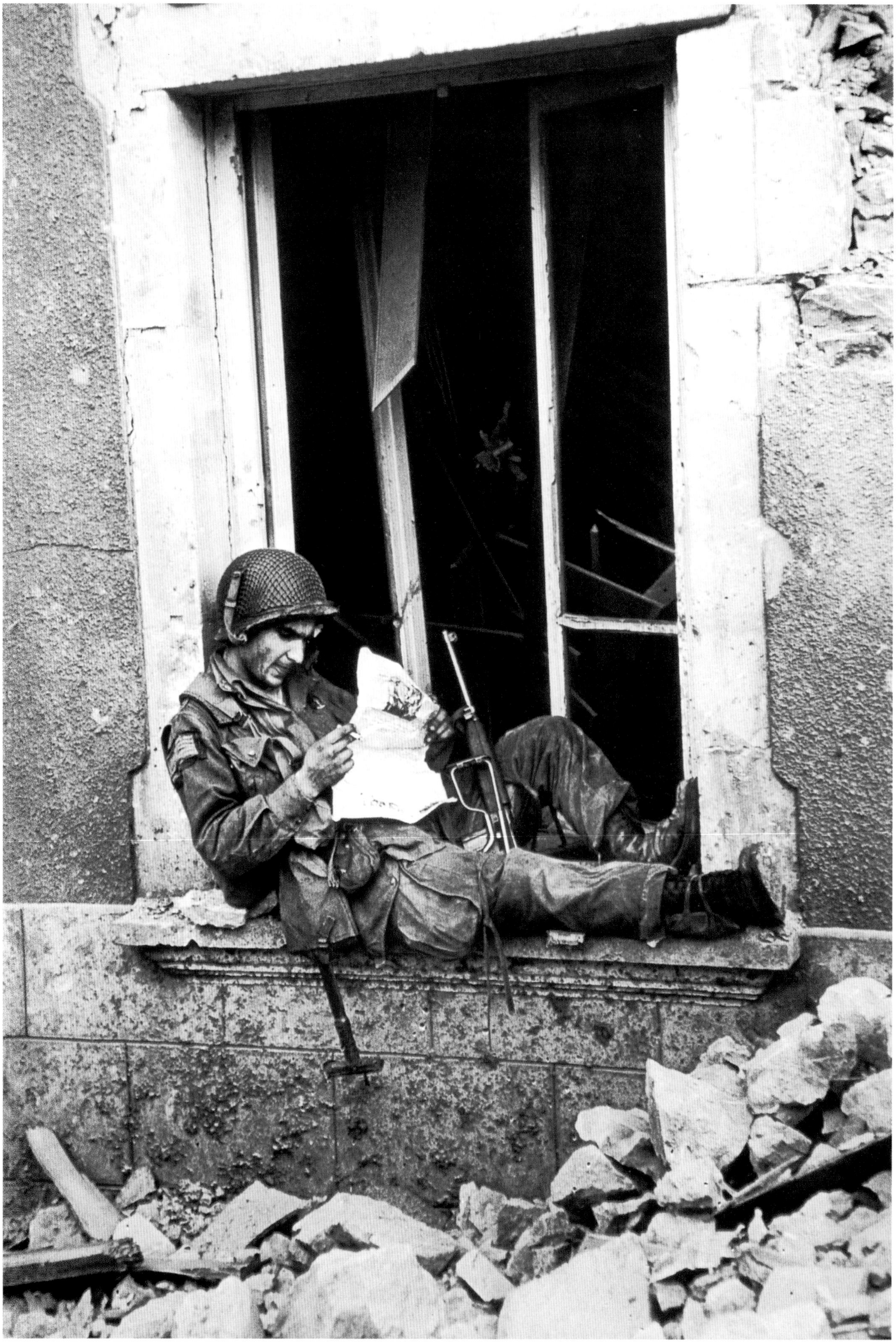

CHAPTER 8 THE AIRBORNE TROOPS' ARMAMENT

No official document exists detailing the issue of weapons to the airborne soldier on the eve of D-Day. The most recent Parachute Infantry Rifle Company Table of organization and equipment (TO & E) 7.37 was dated 24 February 1944.

It became outdated very quickly because of the many modifications which occurred later and were not included in official TO & Es before the landings. Only approximate and unofficial sources can be relied on, but it can however be ascertained that on the whole the airborne troops' weapons were more or less the same as those issued to regular units. The pistol had been taken back from all parachute infantry rifle squad members by the Feb. 1944 T/O, some soldiers however managed to retain this sidearm.

Above.
Love of animals or the hope of a good rabbit stew? The man on the left is armed with an early Thompson M-1928 SMG with cooling fins on the barrel and the Cutts compensator. Under his left arm, note the M1911A1 pistol in its shoulder holster. The First Sergeant has the more common M1A1 Thompson (1942) that he is entitled to as senior company NCO. The two men have cut camouflage neckerchiefs from a piece of parachute canopy.
(National Archives)

Previous page.
At Saint-Sauveur-le-Vicomte, a paratrooper from the 82nd Airborne Div. armed with the M1A1 folding stock carbine. Note the M-1910 shovel with shortened handle and the parachute first aid pocket tied to his jump boot. Wide strips of felt placed under the belt suspender relieve the shoulders. The flag has been stitched onto a piece of cloth before being sewn onto the sleeve.
(Photo R. Capa, collection of the international Center of photography, New York)

Compared with non-airborne units, what was really noticeable was the abundance of so-called weapons for each and every need: knives and pistols, regulation or otherwise, all types of grenades, British-made (mainly) light anti-tank mines; all this turned each infantryman into a walking arsenal.

The basic weapons in the parachute infantry rifle squad were the excellent Garand M1 semi-automatic rifle and the .30 caliber light machine gun (the M-1918 BAR automatic rifle was used only by glider troops). Some Springfield M-1903 rifles with grenade launchers, as well as some M-1903A4s sniper rifles with telescopic sights can be seen on pictures. There was one bazooka at Company HQ and one with the squad command post.

The US M1A1 Carbine

The carbine was mainly issued to officers, and enlisted men whose mission was not close quarters combat, as well as to the parachute infantry rifle squad light machine gunner. A closer study will be made of the M1A1, which at the time was the only shoulder weapon made specifically for paratroopers.

After 1942, the airborne units asked for a more compact version of the regular M1 carbine for parachute artillerymen, engineers and signalmen. The carbine had been adopted to replace the rifle or sidearm for personnel who were not to be hindered by a large gun while they went about their job. Springfield Arsenal, Winchester and the Inland division of General Motors presented different projects, and Inland's design was chosen. The main change consisted of cutting the stock just after the breech and fitting a wooden pistol grip. A tubular metal stock was held to the grip by means of an articulated joint and could be folded over the left-hand side of the carbine. A large number of folding stocks were made by the 'Royal Typewriter' company. Inland was thus able to assemble more than 140,000 M1A1 carbines. The folding stock surplus was delivered to the Ordnance Dept. and to airborne units to repair and convert regular carbines: this explains why there are paratrooper carbines bearing other manufacturer markings than Inland's.

1. Rifle bayonets: M-1942 (long blade) and M1 (short). Both were carried irrespectively and were fitted to the M1 Garand and M-1903 rifles.

2. Padded sheath ('Griswold' bag) for carrying the M1 rifle, dismantled in two parts for the drop. It could also be used for the Thompson and M3 SMGs. The strap and the snap hook enabled it to be fastened to a ring on the parachute harness. On 6 June 1944 however, some paratroopers jumped with the gun assembled and ready to fire, slung over their necks and under the arm, muzzle down.

3. Dismantled M1 Garand Rifle ready to be put in its sheath.

4. M7 Grenade launcher for the M1 rifle.

5. Mk II fragmentation grenade, with the Grenade, Projection adapter for launching it from the rifle (4).

6. Signal, Ground, Parachute (flare rifle grenade).

7. M9A1 Anti-tank Rifle Grenade and its cardboard container.

8. Eight-round M1 rifle clip, caliber .30-06 (7.62 mm), and cardboard cover used in the bandoleer (below).

9. Expendable cotton bandoleer for six rifle clips. Not shown here, the cartridge belt was the ten-pocket regular issue ('Belt, Cartridge, Cal.30, Dismounted M-1923').

However, some paratroopers chose the mounted troops cartridge belt, who had a space for a pistol magazine pocket (fig. 3 page 84) on the left-hand side.

(Photo Militaria Magazine)

Above.
M1 Rifle, Mk II Fragmentation grenade, bandoleer and pockets filled to bursting with ammunition of all sorts, this paratrooper is weighed down. Rifle clips are also carried in the M-1923 rifle belt, which supports the regular first aid packet pouch and canteen. These elite troops had to be able to confront all types of threats and at the same time fight far from the Army's very powerful logistical supply system.
(Reconstruction)

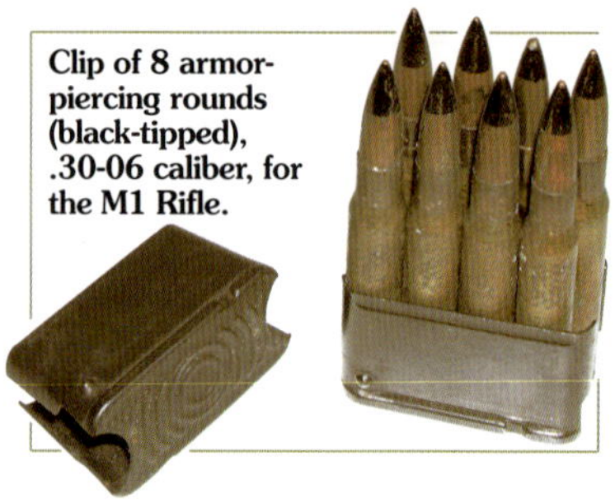

Clip of 8 armor-piercing rounds (black-tipped), .30-06 caliber, for the M1 Rifle.

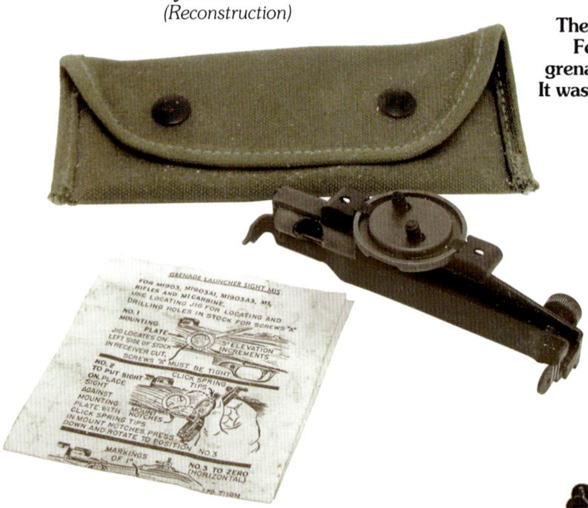

The M-15 sight was adopted in February 1944 for firing rifle grenades (fig. 4, opposite page). It was screwed onto the left-hand side of the rifle stock.

Opposite.
The principal weapons issued to airborne troops.
Left: a Technician NCO of the 82nd A/B division has laid his M1A1 Thompson machine gun against a wall. The extra magazines are carried in a special bag worn over the shoulder. He has hooked a fragmentation Mk II grenade and a Mk III A1 grenade onto the suspender straps. The M3 knife with plastic scabbard is tied to his calf.
In the center a glider pilot, armed with an M1 Rifle. As well as the ten clips contained in the M-1923 cartridge belt, he has a bandoleer with six extra clips.
On the right, knocked out from exhaustion, an officer has placed his M1A1 carbine beside him. He is wearing a gas detection armband, unusual for the 82nd A/B division.
(Reconstruction)

Below.
The M1 Garand US Rifle, adopted in 1936: this semi-automatic .30-06 caliber weapon was the basic rifle unit weapon, used by the infantry and the Engineers. It was powerful and reliable, although it had to be serviced regularly. It was fed with 8-round clips.
(HP Enjames collection, GI Collector Guide)

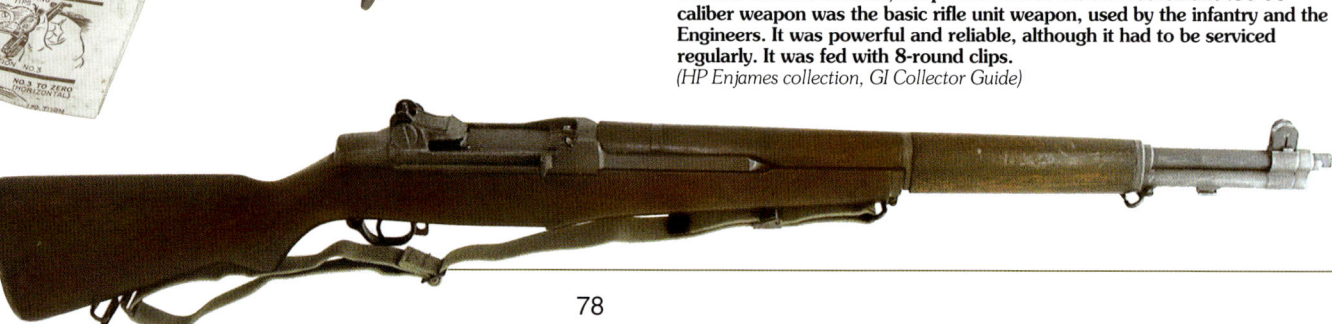

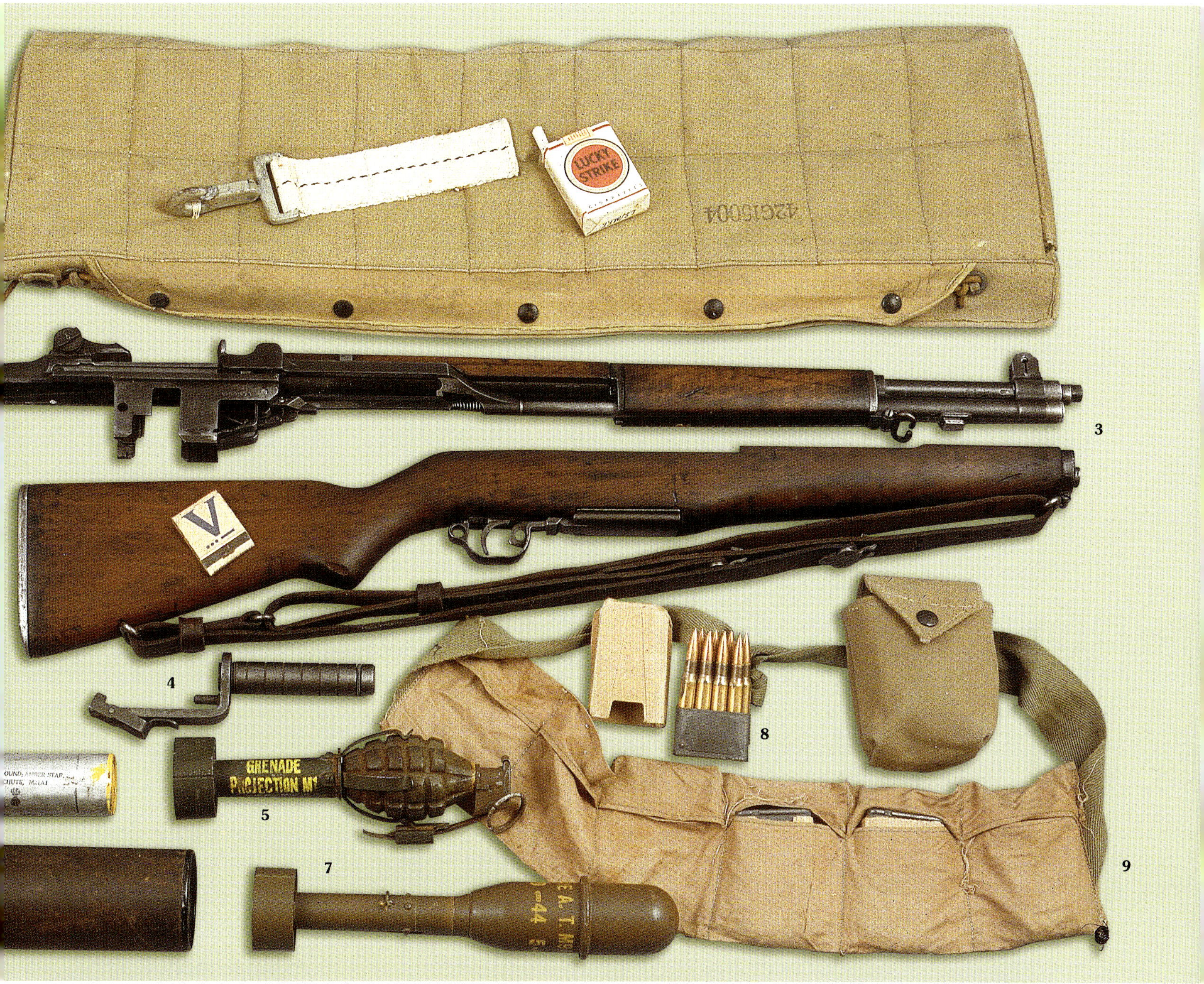
LUCKY STRIKE
3
4
8
GRENADE
PROJECTION M1
5
7
9

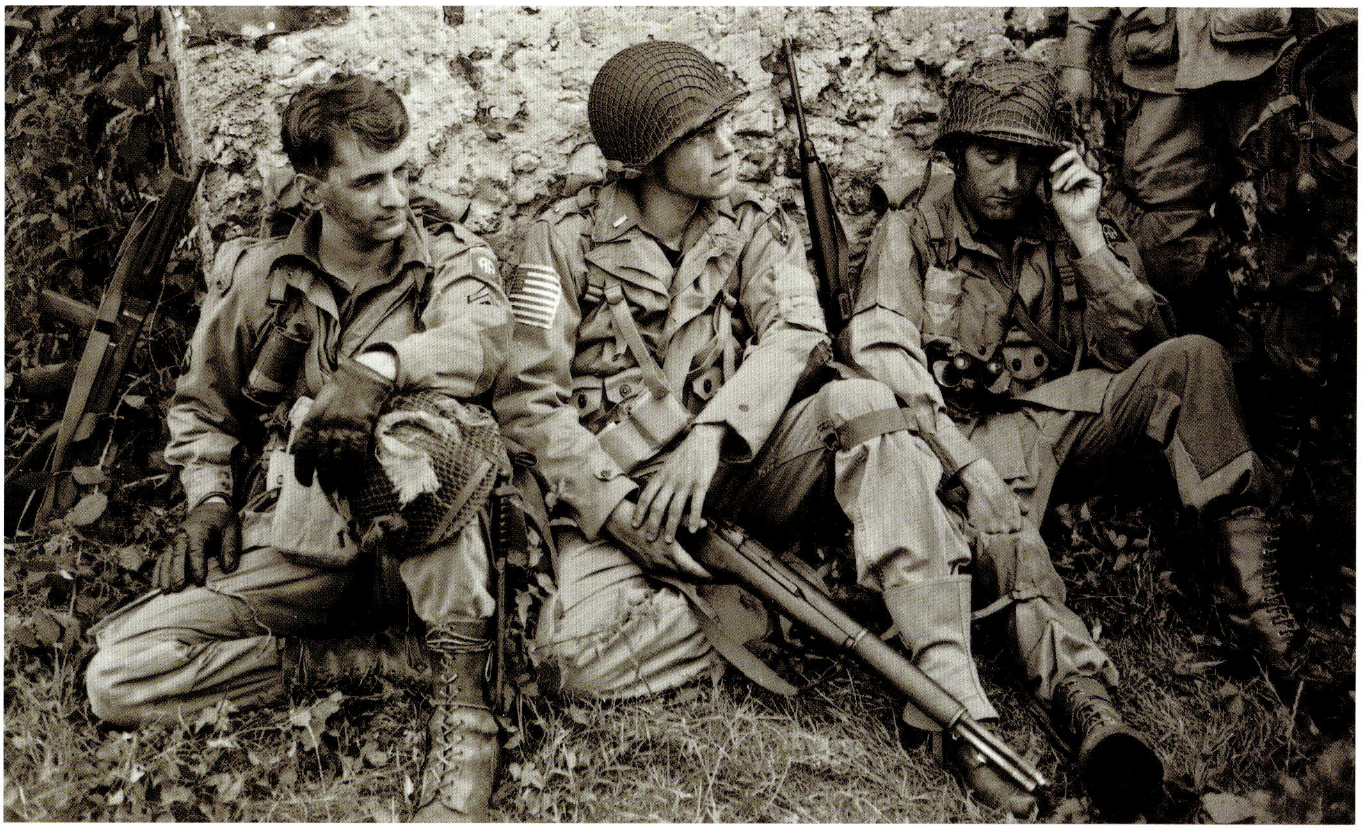

80

1. **USAAF Ammunition Pocket**, diverted for the paratroopers' special needs. They were indexed in the USAAF Catalogue of 30 September 1943 under the designation 'Holder Rifle Clip' for the smaller one, containing four Garand rifle clips, and 'Holder Sub-Machine Gun' for the larger, which held four SMG magazines. They were indeed general purpose pouches and were more versatile than the various issue ammunition belts and carriers. Slipped on the pistol belt, they held greater quantities of ammunition, including grenades. Similar pouches were made in England by parachute riggers, whose flap was fastened by a length of shroud line. The original USAAF version closed with a 'lift the dot' nickel-plated fastener. Another version had the 'Durable' press stud (shown here).
2. **US Carbine M1** (cal .30) and its two 15-round magazine pouch fitted on to the butt.
3. **Pocket, Magazine, double, Web** for the carbine.
4. **US Carbine M1A1** with folding metal stock. Note the oiler in the riveted reinforcement plate half-way along the stock.
5. **M1A1 Carbine jump case.** A loop on the back enabled it to be carried on the belt. The lower strap was used to tie it along the right calf.

(Photo Militaria Magazine)

Right.
Close-up of the breech block and the stock folding system on a US Carbine M1A1 made by the Inland division of General Motors.
(Photo Militaria Magazine)

Below.
This Technician 5th Grade has chosen a Thompson M1A1 sub-machine gun instead of the issue carbine.
The M3 knife in its M6 leather scabbard has been typically strapped to the leg. He also has private-purchase civilian gloves.
(Reconstruction)

The US Carbine

Previous page, bottom.
Items recovered from the battlefield in the eighties. An M1A1 carbine with its carrying case, two M3 fighting knives with their plastic M8 scabbards, a privately-bought Finnish hunting knife, a slide-rule for calculating the load distribution in a CG-4 Waco glider, an 82nd A/B division shoulder patch, a 101st A/B cricket and a compass, are all displayed here on a light stretcher issued to airborne troops.
(Private collection)

Other individual Weapons

Thompson and M3 'Grease gun' sub-machine guns were normally found among the Rifle Company CP personnel, but they were also given to Pathfinders, for instance. Sub-machine guns and M1 rifles were very often preferred by officers to the carbine, whose stopping power was deemed too weak for infantry combat.

US paratroopers carried a huge variety of knives of civilian and military origin (including US Navy fighting knives), as well as machetes, which were not just used on vegetation... Apart from the regulation models, Navy and Signal Corps (a 1917-18 model with an engraved leather scabbard) machetes were also used, as were a host of other obsolete patterns. The close-combat weapon par excellence, 'cold steel' was not only there to give the soldier confidence: the paratroopers knew how to use it and often did so.

The last-resort weapon was still the faithful .45 caliber Colt pistol. It had been given to all parachute infantry squad members in February 1942 then taken back by the February 1944 T/O. But it was to be seen on many a paratrooper in Normandy, either officially issued or purloined from a friendly supply sergeant.

Sub Machine Guns
1. Thompson M1A1 cal. 45 (11.43 mm) sub-machine gun.
2. USAAF-type ammunition pocket, a copy made in Britain by airborne units riggers. It contains here four 20-round magazines for the Thompson sub-machine gun.
3. Issue Thompson SMG magazine bag; on the right a British-made partitioned variant.
4. Sub-machine gun M3 Cal .45 ('Grease gun').
5. M-1918 fighting knife and M6 leather scabbard.
(Photo Militaria Magazine & HP Enjames, GI Collector Guide)

Above.
**With a grimace caused by the effort, this paratrooper climbs with difficulty into the cabin of a C-47, 8-Y coded (98th Squadron/440th Troop Carrier Group). Including the 150 machines lent to British airborne troops, more than a thousand of these twin-engined planes took part in the D-Day operations. The number 1 in chalk near the cargo door indicates this was a lead ship.
The man is armed with the Thompson sub-machine gun and an M3 knife in its M6 leather scabbard laced to his leg.**
(National Archives)

82

3

2

4

83

1. M1911 A1 Pistol in a shoulder holster (normally reserved for officers, USAAF or armor crews).

2. M1911 A1 Pistol in the M-1916 holster.

3. Pocket for two 7-round 11.43 mm clips for the Colt (Pocket Magazine Double, Web M-1923). Older WW1 pockets with a rounded flap were also used.

4. British-made Hawkins ATK 75 Mk III light anti-tank mine.

5. US M18 Smoke Grenade. In this case the smoke would have been red to signal to friendly troops.

6. US Mk II fragmentation Grenade.

7. Demolition charge (TNT half-pound block).

8. Ammunition bag, M1 for carrying rifle clips, magazines, grenades, rifle grenades, etc. The strap was the M-1936 field bag's.

9. USAAF-type ammunition pouch containing two Mk II grenades or four Thompson magazines.

10. British No 82 (Gammon) Grenade.

(Photo Militaria Magazine)

M1911 A1 Caliber .45 Pistol
(HP Enjames collection, GI Collector Guide)

84

Above, right.
The angle of this photograph gives a clear idea of how the different items of equipment were carried during operations. As was often the practice at the time, the M2 helmet's leather chin cup and its straps have been folded up and fastened to the inside of the liner one way or another.
(Reconstruction)

Right.
Captain Robert Piper, 505th PIR, 82nd A/B division, is holding an M3 SMG. It was nick-named 'Grease gun' because it vaguely resembled the vehicle maintenance tool. Compared with the Thompson sub-machine gun, it was yet not a very common weapon in fighting units. Behind the officer, the fuselage of a British Horsa glider can be seen, with part of the perforated ramp for unloading jeeps and cannon out.
(National Archives)

85

Above.
This paratrooper from the 506th PIR, 101st Airborne division has very wisely placed the cumbersome bazooka in a British kit bag. It was strapped to the leg during the jump and held on by a coiled rope, then let out just before landing in order to reduce the paratrooper's weight on contact with the ground. His rifle has been slipped into a mounted troops leather scabbard. The man behind him is armed with an M3 sub-machine gun held under the parachute chest pack.
(National Archives)

Edged Weapons

1. M-1942 rifle bayonet.
2. M1 rifle bayonet.
3. 21 inch-long M-1939 Machete with leather sheath.
4. M-1942 Machete with canvas sheath and leather variant.
5. M3 fighting knife with US M6 plastic scabbard.
6. M3 fighting knife with two M6 leather scabbard variants.
7. M-1918 Trench Knife with its original crimped metal sheath.
8. M2 switchblade knife. It was placed in a zippered pocket bellow the jump jacket collar and was intended for cutting through the parachute rigging in emergencies (and not the harness straps as was thought).

(Photo Militaria Magazine)

87

LIGHT INFANTRY WEAPONS

M-1918 A2 Automatic Rifle (BAR - Browning Automatic Rifle)

This late WW1-vintage automatic rifle was the glider infantry rifle squad light automatic weapon. Fed by 20-round .30 caliber magazines, its rate of fire could reach 500 rounds per minute and this gave powerful interdiction or covering fire. At the end of the muzzle, the bipod steadied the gun's aim and could be removed to lighten the weapon.

Opposite.
M-1938 belt for BAR magazines. BAR team ammunition bearers carried extra magazines in the M1 ammunition bag (fig. 8 page 84).
(HP Enjames collection, GI Collector Guide)

Bazooka (Rocket launcher M1A1)

This anti-tank rocket launcher was found at the infantry units' CPs, among others.
It was 59-mm caliber and could pierce 120-mm armor at a range of 230 feet.
(Coll. Sacleux)

More items recovered from the Normandy battlefield: M2 switchblade knife, 101st Airborne division cricket, American knuckleduster, 101st Airborne division shoulder patch. It had never been sewn on and was given by a paratrooper to a French civilian.
(Private collection)

88

Browning M-1919A4, .30 Caliber Machine gun

Light machine gun used during the whole war: this weapon was issued to all the infantry battalions for D-Day (paratroopers and glider troops). The 'heavy' version (M-1917 A1) was a water-cooled machine gun fitted with a large water-cooling sleeve over the barrel, together with a larger mount.
(HP Enjames collection, GI Collector Guide)

The .30 caliber light machine gun (late-war version, with bipod).
(National Archives)

Browning .50 Caliber M2 Machine Gun

The legendary Browning .50 caliber machine gun was the most powerful heavy automatic weapon used by the infantry units. Although its weight (83 lbs) made it hard to move around on difficult terrain, it gave considerable firepower.
The machine gun at right is on an anti-aircraft mount, it was issued to the AA units of the airborne divisions and brought in by glider.

Below.
Ammunition box for the .50 caliber machine gun.
(HP Enjames collection, GI Collector Guide)

The 60-mm M2 Mortar

The 60-mm M2 Mortar was issued to airborne infantry regiments. It could fire explosive shells or flares at about a mile range. Parachute infantrymen routinely carried ammunition for this weapon.

Right.
60-mm high explosive shell and its carrier tube made of bituminized cardboard.
(HP Enjames collection, GI Collector Guide)

Below.
60-mm mortar crew training in England. These men equipped with a haversack are not paratroopers.
(National Archives)

Above.
Fighting hard as soon as they landed on France, these paratroopers from the 507th PIR, 82nd A/B division are taking a moment's respite. The private on the left is armed with an M1 Rifle with fixed M1 bayonet. He is carrying a bandoleer with six 8-round rifle clips and two Mk II A1 frag. grenades (the yellow stripe indicates live ammunition).
The Parachutist's first aid packet can be tied by its four tapes where most practical, this time on the left arm.
The paratrooper on the right, whose neck is protected by a scarf cut from a parachute canopy, has hooked his last fragmentation grenade to a ring of his M-1936 belt suspender.
(Reconstruction)

The 81-mm M1 Mortar

The Heavy Weapons Company of the parachute and glider-borne infantry battalion was equipped with the 81-mm M1 mortar. This gave longer range support fire (2,750 to 3,300 yards).
(HP Enjames collection, GI Collector Guide)

M4 sight for 60- and 81-mm mortars. The leather carrying case is hooked on to the belt or slung thanks to an adjustable leather strap.
(HP Enjames collection, GI Collector Guide)

91

CHAPTER 9 THE EQUIPMENT

THE AIRBORNE troops' equipment was basically the same as that of other army fighting units. There were however numerous accessories which were specifically issued to the parachute units.

Wherever possible, the official designation is used for all the articles appearing in the Supply Catalog of the QMC or the USAAF Catalog.

Above.
5 June 1944. General Eisenhower, Supreme Commander of the Allied Forces in Europe visited the paratroopers of the 101st A/B. Although they have not yet put their parachutes on, the men are carrying most of their equipment. The paratroopers have tied their recently-issued cloth-printed maps around their left shoulder. The center paratrooper has slipped large pieces of felt under the strap of his bag.
(National Archives)

1. Parachute first-aid packet, see page 100.

2. Bag, canvas, field M-1936. This was carried on the back together with the M-1936 belt suspenders, or over the shoulder by means of an extra strap hooked to the two buckles. The 'musette' bag was issued to all airborne troops. On the other hand, the M-1928 haversack was carried by glider troops who came by sea as reinforcements. The M-1936 bag contained toilet gear, three days' worth of K-rations, a skull cap or M-1941 knit cap, D-rations, a spoon and miscellaneous personal items.
The example shown here on which the identification discs have been placed has been roughly camouflaged with brown paint, which was common practice among the invasion troops.

3. Under the D-type rations (described in 4), are two K-rations, Breakfast and Dinner; the Supper menu is missing. They consisted of a dietetically balanced meal. The small glass bottle contains water purification tablets.

4. Type D survival ration. Every soldier gets 3 three waxed cartons each containing a 4-oz. bar made of chocolate, cocoa butter, solidified skimmed milk, sugar, flour and various vitamins. Three D-bars gave a total of 1,800 calories. This type of ration was intended to boost energy for a period not exceeding three consecutive days.

5. Invasion currency printed in England and in the USA and handed to Allied troops to pay for their purchases in France.

6. Gloves, Horsehide, riding unlined. These were general issue to officers and all parachute personnel, to protect their hands during the drop.

7. Skull cap worn under the helmet concurrently with the woolen M-1941 knit cap. It was either an Air Force mechanic's cap, or a homemade knit item that had been mailed by the family or offered by a charity.

8. M4 lightweight gas mask with M10 A1 filter canister, carried in the M6 bag which also contained the plastic protective cover (9), eyeshields (10), waterproofing kit (11) and two gas detection armbands (12) as well as a tube of decontamination compound (not seen here).

9. Protective cover against liquid vesicants (Cover, protective, individual). It has been taken out of its sealed packaging and has a transparent part for seeing through.

10. Eyeshields, M1. Copied from a British pattern, they came either transparent or tinted and were often used as dust goggles.

11. Kit, gas mask, waterproofing, M1.

12. Sleeve gas detector: this British-made armband was made of thick light brown paper, impregnated with a chemical product whose color turned to blue or pink depending on the type of gas. It was reinforced around the edges by a strip of cloth which formed a loop for the jacket shoulder strap. The gas detection armband was universal issue to invasion troops and not only to airborne soldiers.

13. Assault Gas Mask M5, Filter M11, Bag M7. For the Normandy invasion, all first-wave troops, both sea- and air-borne, were issued with this lightweight mask in a waterproof bag, which was collected after the assault phase and replaced by the regular mask (8).

93

This gear layout represents what one US paratrooper could have carried with him on the night of 5 June.
Most of these items are described in the following pages, but it may be helpful to give further details about some of them:
On the left, on the Air Force 'Vest, Life preserver, B-4;' M-1938 wire cutters in their canvas carrier; – below left, a small brush for cleaning weapons and a waterproof plastic matchbox.
(Photo Militaria Magazine)

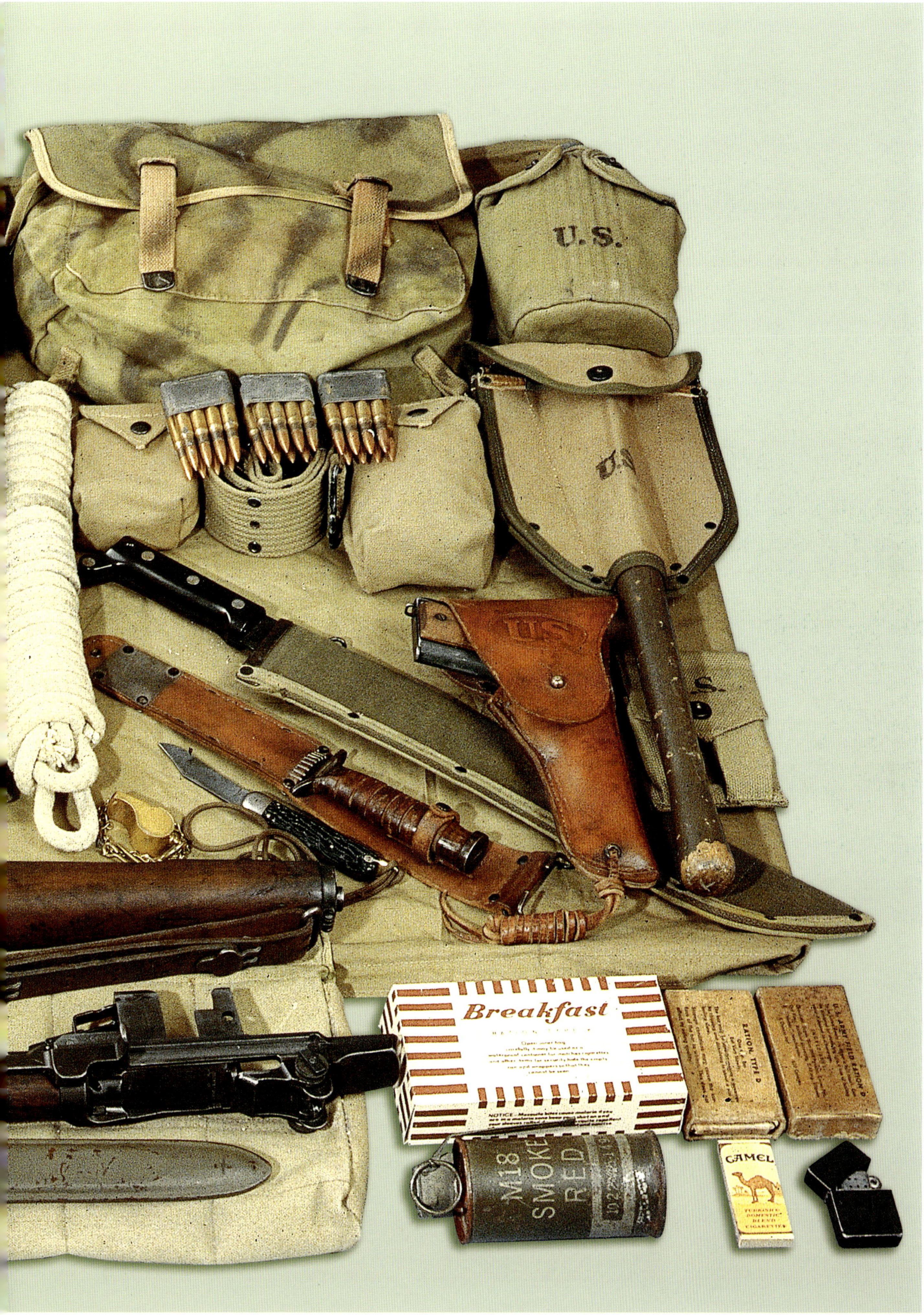
U.S.
U.S.
Breakfast
M18
SMOKE
RED
CAMEL

Optical & Signal Equipment

1. Flare pistol AN-M8; British Verey pistols were also used.

2. Army binoculars (Binoculars M3, 6 x 30) and their leather 'Case, Carrying M-17.'

3. Signal Lamp M-227 and its canvas case. This was battery-operated and enabled different-colored signals to be sent. It could be used from the shoulder or operated from a distance on a tripod. The signals were then sent by means of the Morse-type key and several yards of cable. This installation enabled the signalman to operate the lamp while sheltering from enemy fire should the signals be seen.

4. TL-122 electric torch with a green lens.

5. Single-frequency portable SCR-536 'Handie-talkie' radio, battery- and voice-operated only, switched on by the telescopic aerial. It weighed six pounds and had a maximum range of 1,650 yards. In practice, this was reduced by obstacles such as hedges, hills or buildings.

6. Map Case (Dispatch case M-1938) comprising a plastic sheath to protect documents; there were gussets under the flap for rulers, crayons, etc.

All items here have been placed on a map of the Utah sector and the 82nd and 101st divisions drop zones.
(Photo Militaria Magazine)

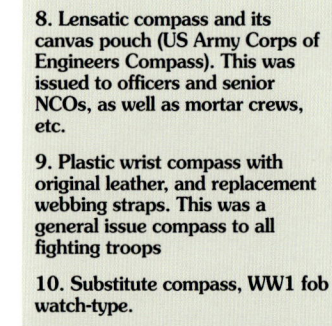

Luminous Markers, Radioactive, Type I in their storage box containing 24. This Corps of Engineers item was attached to the soldier's clothing or gear when marching at night, or on any piece of equipment to make finding it at night easier.
(Private collection)

Opposite page.

7. Escape kit. Originally meant for airforce crews, this brown paper envelope contains a map of Normandy printed on cloth, a miniature metal saw, money, small compass (see page 65). For obvious reasons of security, this pocket was only issued when the two divisions were assembled in their embarkation zones. Unless they held a special pass, nobody could enter or leave.

8. Lensatic compass and its canvas pouch (US Army Corps of Engineers Compass). This was issued to officers and senior NCOs, as well as mortar crews, etc.

9. Plastic wrist compass with original leather, and replacement webbing straps. This was a general issue compass to all fighting troops

10. Substitute compass, WW1 fob watch-type.

11. Brass and war time plastic whistles, used by officer and NCOs for rallying and giving orders. It was put in the left breast pocket and the chain attached to the shoulder strap.

12. Government issue wristwatch.
(Photo Militaria Magazine)

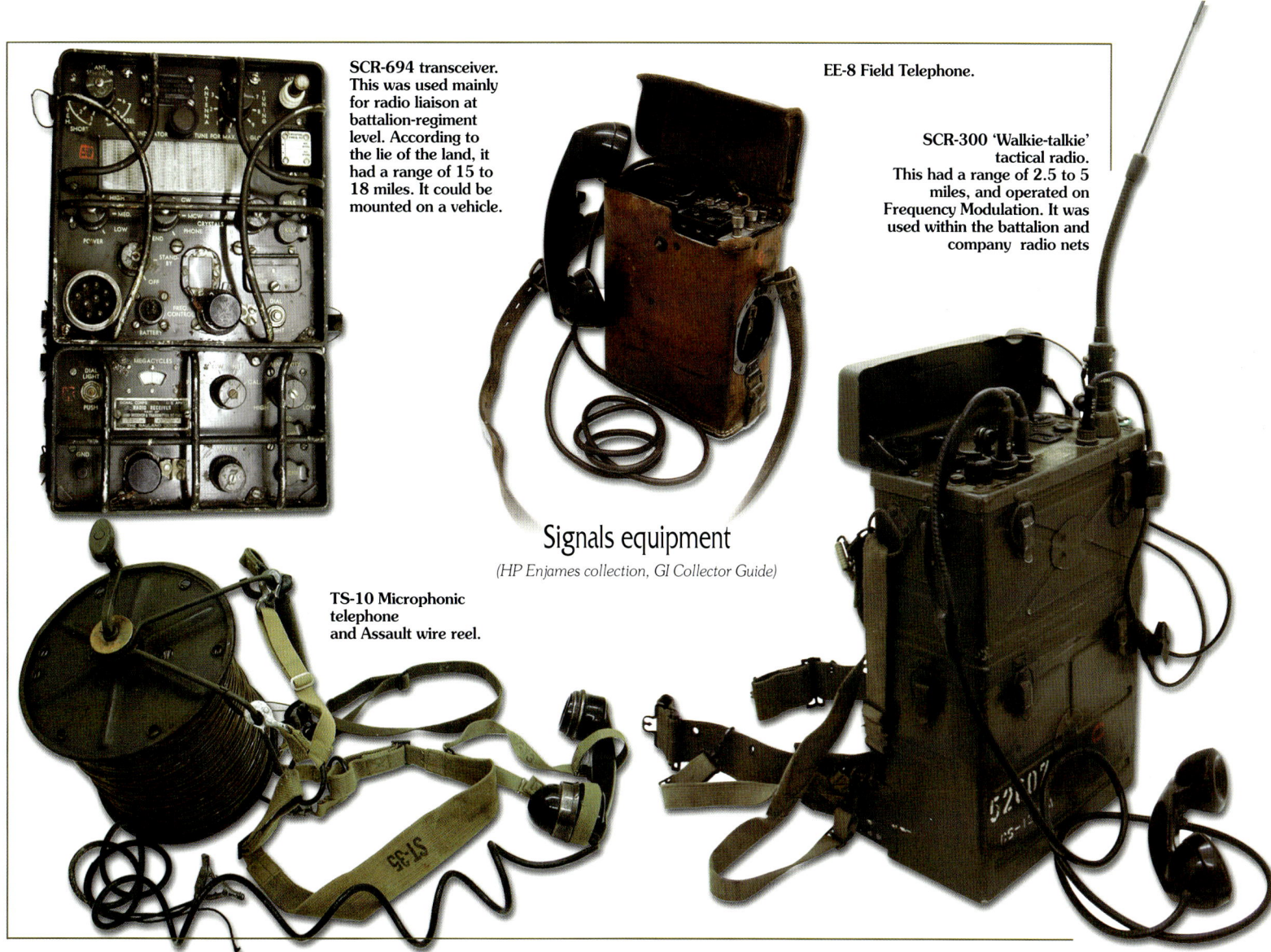

SCR-694 transceiver. This was used mainly for radio liaison at battalion-regiment level. According to the lie of the land, it had a range of 15 to 18 miles. It could be mounted on a vehicle.

EE-8 Field Telephone.

SCR-300 'Walkie-talkie' tactical radio. This had a range of 2.5 to 5 miles, and operated on Frequency Modulation. It was used within the battalion and company radio nets

Signals equipment
(HP Enjames collection, GI Collector Guide)

TS-10 Microphonic telephone and Assault wire reel.

Topographical and escape equipment

THE CONTAINERS

The A-5 container (Parapack)

Intended to be dropped at the same time as the paratroopers or during reinforcement and supply missions, the A-5 Container brought in equipment which was too heavy to be carried by the men: weapons such mortars and heavy machine guns, ammunition, radios and medical supplies. It was attached under the belly of the aircraft or simply dropped from the cargo door.

The A-5 Container was divided into three parts:
– The central part was made up of a padded rectangular cover (made up from several M1 rifle jump cases, 'Griswold bags') undone and stitched together, simply rolled around the equipment to be dropped.
– Two end pieces made of reinforced padded canvas were attached at the end of the cover by straps fitted with rings and snap hooks.
– The parachute bag was attached to one end of the container, the two elevators being connected to each of the end pieces. When the canopy opened, the container was in an almost horizontal position. There was a padded cushion to absorb the shock when it reached the ground.

The color of the parachute canopy revealed what was in the container: blue - K rations, green - fuel, red or yellow - ammunition or explosives, white - medical or signals equipment.

Opposite.
These paratroopers are training to stow an A-5 container under a C-47 transport plane.
Six of these could be carried under the belly. Containers of arms, ammunition and equipment could be dropped at the same time as the paratroopers.
(National Archives)

Below.

The A-5 container
Unlike the British, the American Airborne used 'soft' containers. Similar containers to this one were used for dropping larger matériel such as the 75-mm pack howitzer. It was dismantled and packed in six bundles.
But in the dark, because the bundles got dispersed and because of the enemy, the 377th PFABn of the 101st A/B division was only able to set up one such gun on 6 June.
(HP Enjames collection, GI Collector Guide)

Lamp Assembly Identification Aerial Delivery Container.
Light beacon for signaling the position of containers dropped by night.
The colors of the filters indicated the type of load.
(HP Enjames collection, GI Collector Guide)

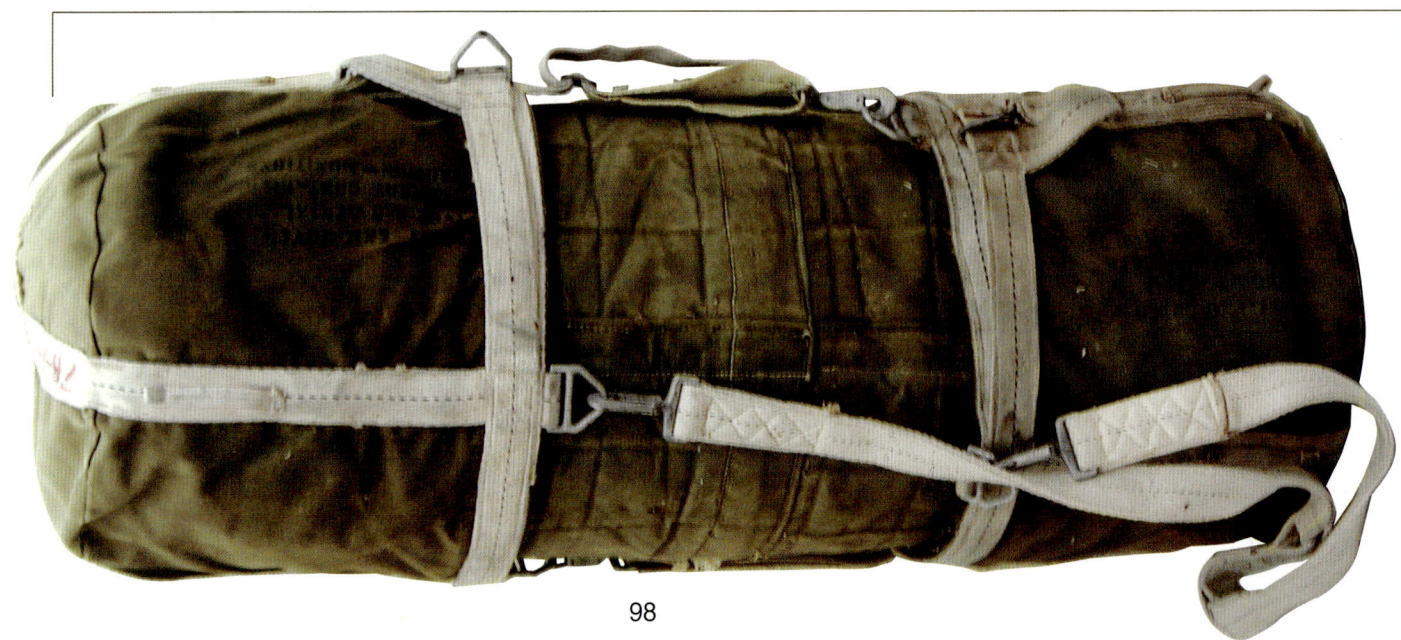

Above.
5 June in the afternoon, in front of the C-47 'Lady Lillyan,' first lieutenant Alex Bobuck of HQ Co. 3/506 of the 101 A/B division checks the equipment of his men before loading. He is carrying an unidentified hand gun under his belt.
The paratrooper facing him carries pigeon containers. Note the sergeant's stripes painted on the sleeve of the man in the center: although forbidden, this was common practice. Our man actually seems to have tied a map-case onto his right leg.
On the C-47, the black and white invasion stripes have been applied hastily round the USAAF star.
(National Archives)

Opposite.
'Mae West' life jackets have been taken out of storage for imminent issue to airborne troops. Despite this precaution, they were of no use whatsoever to the men who fell into the flooded areas near the rivers Dives and Merderet. Weighed down by their equipment and all tangled up in their parachute harness, many of them drowned in shallow water.
(National Archives)

MEDICAL SUPPLIES

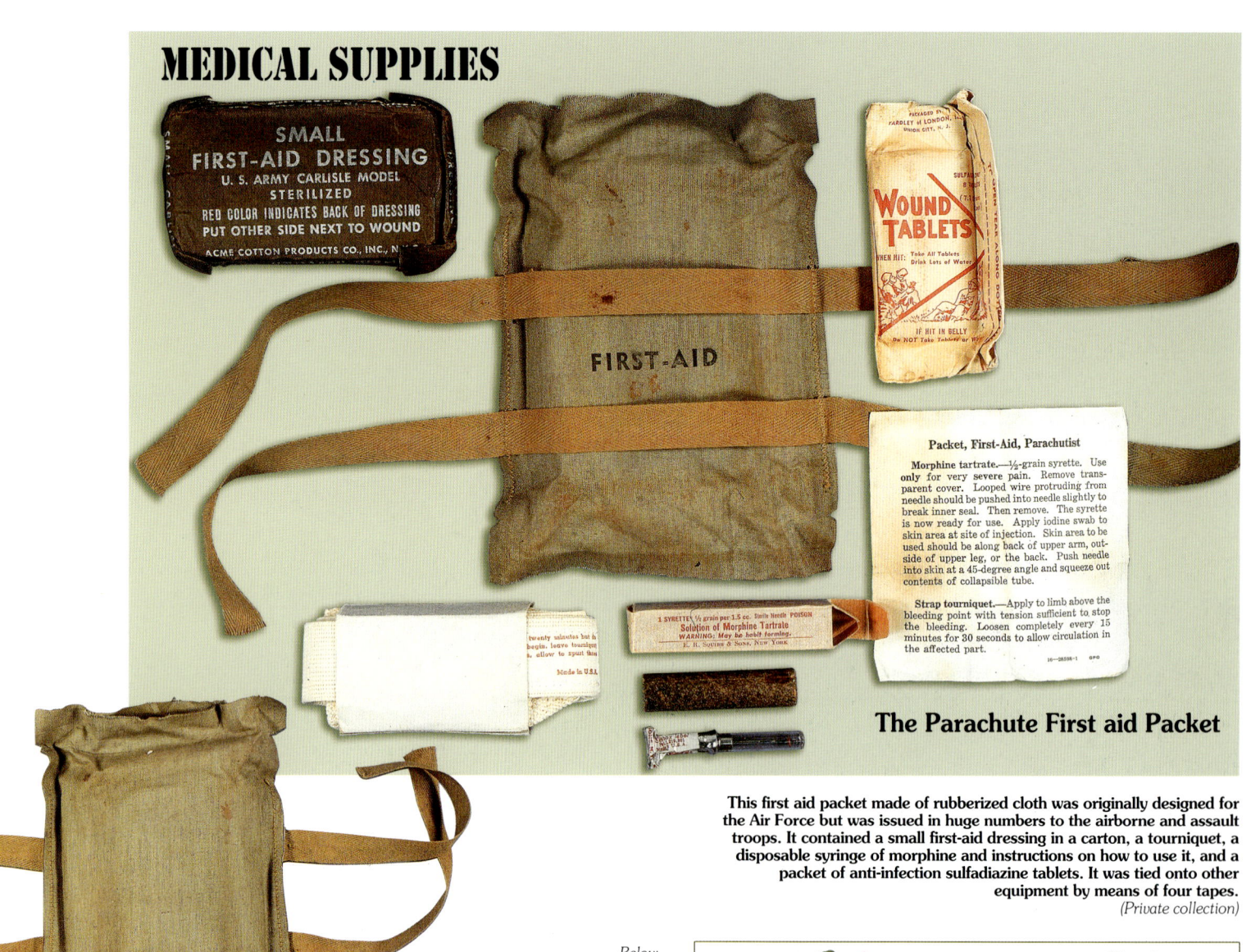

The Parachute First aid Packet

This first aid packet made of rubberized cloth was originally designed for the Air Force but was issued in huge numbers to the airborne and assault troops. It contained a small first-aid dressing in a carton, a tourniquet, a disposable syringe of morphine and instructions on how to use it, and a packet of anti-infection sulfadiazine tablets. It was tied onto other equipment by means of four tapes.
(Private collection)

Below.
An airborne Medical Corps captain's helmet.
The metal rank bars usually worn on the uniform have here been welded onto the helmet front.
(Musée de la Seconde Guerre mondiale at Ambleteuse)

Equipment for medics

Special suspenders for medics

Medic bag containing first aid supplies. Carried in twos, they could be hung from the harness shown above or to the M-1936 Pistol belt, together with two canteens.
(HP Enjames collection, GI Collector Guide)

Above.
This extraordinary photograph was taken on 6 June, just inland from Utah Beach.
A first aid post and collection point has been set up near the shore by the medical section of an Engineer Special Brigade whose special insignia can be seen on the medic standing up on the right, carefully filling in the evacuation tag. These indicate the nature of each man's wounds, precious indications for the hospital staff to whom the casualties were sent, by sea.
The majority of the wounded seen here are paratroopers. Many were injured on landing or exhausted by a long night of uncertain wandering around, looking for their units and their targets. Many of them are wearing the garrison caps with the airborne insignia.
(National Archives, via JYN)

According to the Geneva Convention, medical personnel and chaplains wore neutrality armbands.
(HP Enjames collection, GI Collector Guide)

Right.
A medic attached to the 3rd Battalion, 501st PIR, 101st A/B division (according to the markings on his helmet, page 56) helps with the loading of wounded aboard a GMC truck which will take them to the beaches, where they will be evacuated to England.
The devotion of the medical teams often in the front line enabled the lives of many of the wounded to be saved. For some the war as over, for others they rejoined their units after healing.
(National Archives)

An M-1910 shovel with the handle shortened to make it less cumbersome, a common practice among the paratroopers.

(Private collection)

'Rigger-Made' bag fitted with a strap for an undetermined use, found in the Briquebec region.

'Rigger-Made' belt pouch for M1 rifle clips or Mk II frag. grenades.

THE CRICKETS

"One click answered by two clicks…" This gadget was made famous by the film 'The Longest Day.'

The only crickets identified on period photographs or found on the battlefield were apparently used solely by the 101st Airborne division. These crickets were bought in a hurry from a British toy-maker, a short while before 6 June 1944. Several 82nd Airborne veterans however insist that they were issued with cricket toys (frogs, cicadas, etc.).

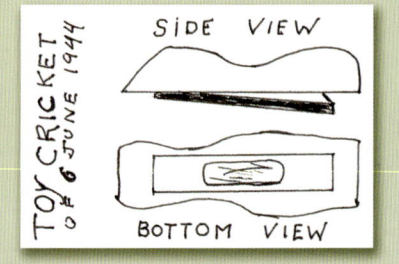

Crickets used by the 101st Airborne division, seen from three different angles. The one on the left has been holed so it could be tied to a string.

A drawing made at our request by Tom Porcella, a veteran of the 508th PIR (82d division) in March 1987. Other veterans confirm having received toy crickets.

An example of the cricket toys that were allegedly issued to elements of the 82nd A/B.

(Private collection)

CHAPTER 10 INSIGNIA AND DECORATIONS

Insignia worn by the American Airborne troops fell into two categories: those which served to identify the soldier in combat and those used to embellish the dress and off-duty uniform.

In combat, apart from rank insignia, airborne soldiers sported the unit patch on the left shoulder and the Stars and stripes flag, more typically within the 82d Division, which was characteristic of amphibious or airborne operations into enemy or enemy-held territory.

The Identification flag

In order to avoid brutal reactions from the enemy if captured and to enable French Civilians to readily identify the liberators and assist them, the High Command had small American Flags distributed on the eve of the landings to be attached to the right arm (as had been done already in North Africa for operation 'Torch' in 1942 and as would be done in Southern France in August 1944).

Period photographs bear witness to the fact that only paratroopers and glider troops of the 82nd Airborne division as well as the glider pilots were issued with them. There were three types of emblem (see the photograph below):

– Fig. 1. Small format 4.7 in x 2.7 in. muslin flag. The damaged borders are narrower than originally.
– Fig. 2. Small format 5.1 in x 2.7 in. made of plasticized cloth, note the machine stitching.
– Fig 3. Large format 5.1 in x 3.8 in. made of plasticized cloth. This was the original armband issued in North Africa, meant to be attached to the sleeve by safety pins. Mainly worn by glider pilots, it had been cut out and stitched to the sleeve.

Shortly before D-day.
From left to right: Privates Downes, Cleaver and Levesque, paratroopers from the 82nd Airborne division, are wandering in a park near Nottingham. Their boots have been painstakingly polished and the characteristic colored oval of the Airborne troops can be seen on the left-hand side of the chest, behind the paratrooper wings. As allowed in the warm season, Cleaver is wearing the flannel shirt, with the tie tucked in between the second and third buttons, as per regulations.
(Tom Porcella)

Small format flag, similar to fig. 1 below. It is sewn on an original jump jacket found near Pont-l'Abbé. Note that the star design has been printed upside down.
(Private collection)

Below.
Three models of identification flags worn on the right hand sleeve, captioned in the text above.
(Photo Militaria Magazine)

Above, left.

THE AIRBORNE ENLISTED MAN'S SERVICE UNIFORM

October 1945. This Technician 4th Grade of the 326th Engineer Battalion (101st Airborne division) has put on his service uniform for the last time before going back to civilian life.
1. Garrison Cap with engineer white and red piping. The generic airborne troops' insignia is sewn to the left-hand side.
2. Coat, Wool, Serge, simplified pattern adopted in 1942.
3. Collar disks: on the right the US monogram, on the left a castle, the Corps of Engineers arm-of-service insignia.
4. Paratrooper wings and ribbon bar. The wings are embroidered on a green cloth background ands this was uncommon for the service uniform. It is most likely that this NCO's original silver wings were given as a souvenir to some charming Parisian girl!

Above, right.

THE AIRBORNE OFFICER'S SERVICE UNIFORM
1. Silver rank bars (also pinned on the shoulder straps).
2. Airborne troops' generic insignia, worn on the right as the regulations stipulated for officers.
3. Officer collar badges. On the collar, the U.S. initials, on the lapels, the crossed rifles of the infantry.
4. Distinguished Unit Citation. This rewarded a whole unit for its exemplary conduct under fire (the 505th PIR was awarded the DUC for its action at Sainte-Mère-Eglise from 6-9 June 1944).
5. Parachutist's wings.
6. Medal ribbons.
7. Combat Infantryman Badge. It was created on 15 November 1943 and was awarded only to infantry officers and men who showed valor and competence in the front line. It entailed a $10 pay bonus. Among the great number of insignia and medals awarded to the soldiers, the CIB was the only one which they considered valuable as it distinguished frontline soldiers from rear-echelon personnel.
8. Overseas stripes were embroidered with yellow thread, or gold bullion; each stripe meant six months' service abroad. Note the bronze colored braid sewn onto the officers' jacket and coat lower sleeve.

Back in England after the battle, this young Captain in the 505th Parachute Infantry Regiment has put on his best uniform before posing for the souvenir shot in a London photographer's. He is wearing the Officer's dark wool gabardine service coat and 'pink' trousers. He is also wearing a non-regulation 'pink' Garrison Cap with black and gold officer piping. The trousers are bloused into the prized jump boots, which were worn in all circumstances. His insignia is described below.
(Reconstruction, photo Militaria Magazine)

104

PARATROOPER AND GLIDER WINGS

THE PARACHUTIST BADGE

It was designed by Captain Yarborough of the 501st PIB (Parachute Infantry Battalion) at the beginning of March 1941, and approved on 10 March 1941. This was awarded to all paratroopers who completed their training at the Fort Benning Parachute Training School.

British-made wings, decorated with three stars. (for the three combat jumps)

British-made wings.

British-made wings.

American-made wings.

American-made wings.

Oval in the colors of the 502nd PIR, embroidered on felt.

American-made wings (the 'Sterling' hallmark indicates silver in the alloy).

British-made, with their characteristic pin.

(Private collection)

Wing Backgrounds

These oval insignia, woven or embroidered according to a definite color code identified each airborne regiment. They were sewn above the left breast pocket of the uniform and served as a background for the para or glider badge. Most of them were only officially authorized after the end of the war (see pages 109-110).

THE GLIDER BADGE

The Glider badge was authorized on 14 March 1944 for Glider-borne troops who had made at least one landing in enemy-held territory. Bronze stars were added for each subsequent operation.

American-made badge.

Reverse of the British-made badge, with its typical pin.

Reverse of the American-made badge above. The pin is held in a typical small rotating lock.

British-made badge (Gaunt's, in London) pinned onto its original cardboard.

(Private collection)

105

GARRISON CAP INSIGNIA

The origin of the Garrison Cap Patches, once again specific to Airborne units, went back to the beginning of 1941. At that time officers of the 501st Parachute infantry battalion insisted that their men be distinguished from the rest of the infantry. They had cloth discs made showing a white parachute on a light blue background (the distinctive color of the infantry, already seen on the cap piping). In the summer of 1942, this initiative was copied by the newly-raised airborne units: there was a design with a red background for the Engineers and the Artillery.

Until 25 April 1942, all units wore the patch on the left hand side of the cap; but from that date, all officers had to wear their rank insignia there, so that the Airborne insignia moved to the right hand side of officers' caps. Certain 'hard nuts' went as far as to pin their rank insignia on the disk on the left hand side. During the summer of 1942, a similar insignia was introduced for the Glider troops with a white embroidered glider flying to the right for the officers and towards the left for enlisted men. Finally during the spring of 1943, the Airborne Command created a single insignia to put an end to all the different variations. The variants were nevertheless kept in spite a multitude of memoranda on the subject.

For almost all the designs mentioned there were fancier models, more often made locally on the initiative of unit commanders where no official insignia existed. Bought from the PX, these were in particular embroidered and other high quality patches for the off-duty uniform.

Parachute infantry garrison cap insignia (light blue branch color)

1   2   3   4   5

Airborne Artillery and Engineers garrison cap patches (branch color: red)

6   7   8   9

1. The earliest patch (blue background without piping) designed by First Lieutenant William T. Ryder commanding the Parachute Test Platoon in 1941.
2. Woven patch.
3. Embroidered on felt.
4. Embroidered on cloth
5. Embroidered in silver bullion (non-regulation in 1944).

Glider Troops garrison cap patches

10   11   12   13   14

Generic airborne troops garrison cap patches (1943)

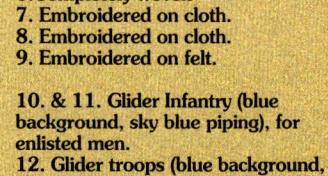

15   16   17

6. Completely woven
7. Embroidered on cloth.
8. Embroidered on cloth.
9. Embroidered on felt.

10. & 11. Glider Infantry (blue background, sky blue piping), for enlisted men.
12. Glider troops (blue background, red piping).
13. and 14. Glider Artillery/Engineers (red background, white piping), officer pattern.
15. Airborne Infantry: blue background, blue piping, enlisted men (glider flying to the left) embroidered on felt.
16. Ditto, completely woven.
17. Airborne Artillery (red background, white piping), for officers (glider flying to the right), embroidered on cloth.

18   19   20   21

18. to 21. Generic Airborne troops patch: blue background, red piping. Fig. 19 was for officers.
(Private collection)

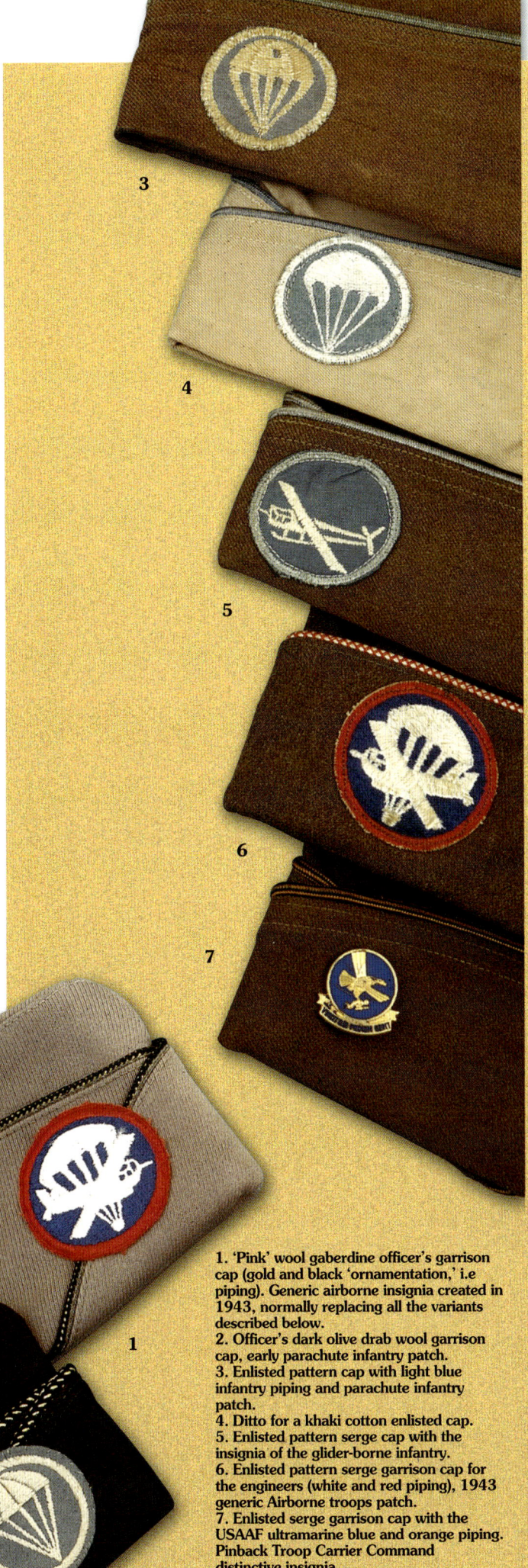

PATHFINDER INSIGNIA

In May 1944 a distinctive insignia was created for the Pathfinders (C-47 crews and paratroopers). The 'Winged Torch' was designed by Lieutenant Prescott (a C-47 navigator) and was approved by Lt.-Col. Crouch, the Pathfinders' CO in the IX Troop Carrier command. Following and order placed in London in a hurry, the first were issued on 5 June 1944! For reasons of security - the Pathfinders' technology being ultra secret - wearing the insignia was forbidden on the combat uniform. The badge was worn on the left forearm of service or going-out dress.

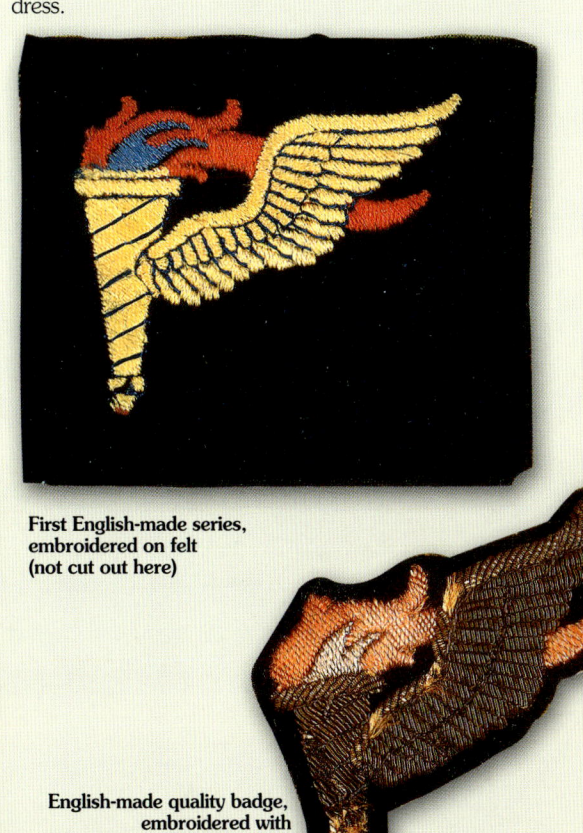

First English-made series, embroidered on felt (not cut out here)

English-made quality badge, embroidered with silver bullion on a felt background.

(Private collection)

1. 'Pink' wool gaberdine officer's garrison cap (gold and black 'ornamentation,' i.e piping). Generic airborne insignia created in 1943, normally replacing all the variants described below.
2. Officer's dark olive drab wool garrison cap, early parachute infantry patch.
3. Enlisted pattern cap with light blue infantry piping and parachute infantry patch.
4. Ditto for a khaki cotton enlisted cap.
5. Enlisted pattern serge cap with the insignia of the glider-borne infantry.
6. Enlisted pattern serge garrison cap for the engineers (white and red piping), 1943 generic Airborne troops patch.
7. Enlisted serge garrison cap with the USAAF ultramarine blue and orange piping. Pinback Troop Carrier Command distinctive insignia.
(Photo Militaria Magazine)

| WEARING AIRBORNE INSIGNIA (1944) ||
INSIGNIA	LOCATION
Shoulder patch (See pages 108-110)	At the top of the left-hand sleeve, 1/2 inch from the shoulder seam. **Officers:** on the winter and summer service coats, on the shirt (when worn by itself), on the greatcoat, sometimes on the field overcoat **Enlisted men:** service coat, shirt (when worn by itself), wool overcoat, field and jump jackets.
Wings, oval and CIB, see pages 105 & 109-110	On the left-hand side of the chest, on the service coat and shirt, exceptionally with the field uniform.
Distinctive Insignia Enameled unit crest (regiment, battalion), see pages 109-111.	**Officers:** shoulder straps of the service coat **Enlisted men:** lapels of the service coat.
Pocket Patches (Non-regulation regiment or battalion embroidered patches, see pages 109-111)	On the left-hand pocket of sports and training clothes. For officers, exceptionally on the field uniform (leather USAAF flying jacket, for instance). Seen sometimes on the enlisted men's wool shirt pockets
Garrison cap insignia See previous page	Olive drab wool or khaki cotton garrison caps: on the right hand side for officers, on the left for enlisted men.
Identification Flag See page 103	At the top of the right sleeve for 82 A/B division personnel and glider pilots. Field uniform only.

The Unit Patch
(Shoulder Sleeve insignia)

These are the divisional patch worn on the left shoulder at the top by the 82nd and 101st Airborne, but also the USAAF generic insignia or the 9th Air Force Patch of the glider pilots and air crews. All these shoulder patches were worn on the field and service uniforms. Regiment or battalion pocket patches were also among unit insignia, worn on officer's flight jackets or the enlisted men's shirt pockets. These were not regulation and in theory not worn in combat.

Worn on the service coat only, Distinctive Insignia were small enameled crests bearing the regiment or battalion's coat of arms. They were pinned onto the officers' shoulder straps and the lapels of the enlisted men's service coat. Given the number of newly-created units, it seems that not all Airborne units them had Distinctive Insignia at the time. Note also that most of the insignia which appear on our tables were only rarely issued, as the War Department had restricted the use of certain strategic metals, such as copper and bronze.

Finally, the officers' collar badges can be considered as unit insignia: they identified the arm-of-service and sometimes the unit when the regiment or battalion number was added underneath. They were pinned on the service coat lapels, and the left shirt collar, both on the field and the service uniform.

**This paratrooper from the 82nd Airborne Division is comforting a wounded prisoner. He has very roughly cross-stitched his unit patch on the jump jacket's left sleeve. The man's name is printed in black using a stencil above the left pocket, a common practice in the airborne divisions.
He has a reinforced uniform and pencils are sticking out from the chest pocket flap. His hands are protected by the issue woolen gloves with leather-reinforced palms.**
(National Archives)

82nd Airborne division Insignia

The insignia was approved in October 1918 and the 'Airborne' tab was added in August 1942 at the time the infantry division was changed into an airborne unit. The two 'A's stuck together are the initials for 'All American' meaning that the men of the 1917 unit came from all the States in the Union.

American-made shoulder patch, found in Normandy.

Three variants of American-made insignia.

Reverse side of the three patches above. On the left, variant with green weave thread, called 'Green back' by collectors.

82ND AIRBORNE DIVISION UNITS INSIGNIA

Pocket Patch of the 508th PIR

Distinctive insignia of the 82nd Airborne Division (Headquarter personnel).

Pocket Patch of the 507th PIR

Officer collar insignia, 508th PIR

Officer collar insignia 320th GFABn

Distinctive insignia, 325th GIR

Distinctive insignia, 319th GFABn

Distinctive insignia, 320th GFABn

Distinctive insignia, 376th PFABn

505th PIR oval, embroidered on heavy cloth.

325th GIR oval, embroidered

Artillery/Engineers oval

101st Airborne division patch

THE DESIGN takes up that of an older Civil War badge, worn by a regiment of the Iron Brigade (made up of men recruited in Wisconsin) and which already had an eagle as its mascot. Its motto was 'Screaming Eagles.
The divisional patch was approved on 29 May 1942, the 'Airborne' was added on 28 August 1942.

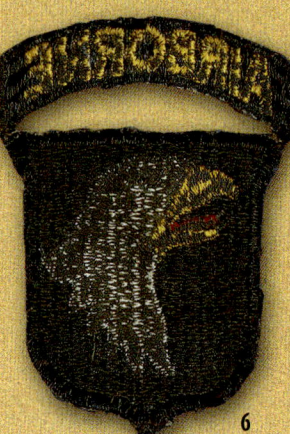

British-made insignia embroidered on a felt background

Top.
This 'Screaming Eagle' from the 101st Airborne division has been captured. In front of the German photographer, his smile is significant because he knows that the roles could soon be reversed. Note the shoulder patch sewn in the regulation spot as well as the rough white thread stitches. No esthetic effect was sought on the combat uniform!
(Bundesarchiv)

1 to 4. Four American-made variants
Note the exceptional variant with a white tongue (4).

5 and 6. The reverse of the two insignia above. On the right, an example embroidered with a green weave thread.

Upottery airfield, 5 June 1944. Privates C.C. Ware and C.R. Plaudo are demolition specialists with the Headquarters Company of the 506th PIR (101st Airborne division). They are touching up their Mohican-style war-paint for the last time. Their hair has also been cut Indian-style. Camouflaging the face was often done with the soot from burnt corks, but also by using black, green or tan cream ordered by the Quartermaster Corps from prominent beauty cream manufacturers. Plaudo has sewn an extra pocket on the sleeve of his jump suit jacket, and the famous 'Screaming Eagle' patch on the flap. The 'Gloves, Horsehide, Riding Unlined' can be clearly seen here, as well as a rigger made pouch on the belt. Under Plaudo's arm, the Signal Corps leather CS-34 case holds a pair of pliers and an electrician's knife. These tools were meant for telephone line repairmen, but were also issued to demolition specialists to prepare explosive charges.
(National Archives)

101st AIRBORNE DIVISION UNITS INSIGNIA

Pocket Patch of the 501st PIR

Pocket Patch of the 506th PIR

Pocket Patch of the 502d PIR

Distinctive insignia, 501st PIR

Distinctive insignia, 506th PIR

Distinctive insignia, 327th GIR

Distinctive insignia, 321st GFABn

Distinctive insignia, 377th PFABn

501st PIR wings oval background, first model worn after 1941, embroidered on heavy cloth.

Officer's collar insignia, 321st GFABn

AIRFORCE FLYING PERSONNEL WINGS

1 - Pilot Wings. Introduced on 25 January 1919 and called the 'Pilot Badge' after 20 February 1940, it was awarded to qualified pilots who had flown at least 200 hours and 75 hours solo. American-made insignia, marked 'Sterling.'
2 - Navigator Wings. Established on 4 September 1942. British-made wings.
3 & 4 - Aircrew Member Wings. Established on 4 September 1942, worn by Troop Carrier mechanics and load/jump masters.
(fig. 3 is American-made and fig. 4 is British-made)
5 & 6 - Glider Pilot Wings (4 September 1942). Awarded to students who had successfully completed the glider pilot's test with CG-4A gliders, including at least three hours' flying and ten landings.
(fig. 5 is American-made and fig. 6 is British-made).

9th Air Force shoulder patch, standard American manufacture

Generic USAAF shoulder patch (US-made early example, embroidered on felt)

9th Air Force shoulder patch with non-regulation 'Airborne' title, hardly worn before D-Day. British-made patch, embroidered on felt.

Airborne Troop Carrier Command patch, worn after August 1944. British-made, embroidered on felt (here taken off a uniform).

9th Air Force patch. British-made, printed on cloth.

1st Troop Carrier Command, non-regulation novelty patch, sold in Post exchanges

LIEUTENANT KIESLING, C-47 PILOT

Pocket insignia for the 1st Troop carrier Command. American-made, embroidered on twill.

1st Troop Carrier Command. American-made, embroidered patch, half size for the garrison cap

Silk-screened on leather chest patch.

Enamel distinctive insignia. American-made pinback. For the garrison cap or service coat.

Souvenirs belonging to Lieutenant Kiesling: identification tags, 1st Troop Carrier Command shoulder patch; distinctive insignia in their original box.

(All items from the collection of the Musée de la Seconde Guerre Mondiale at Ambleteuse, Pas-de-Calais. Photographs by Eric Barbe)

Portrait of Lieutenant Kiesling, a C-47 pilot with the IX Troop Carrier Command.

Service coat and cap belonging to Lieutenant Kiesling.

Post-August 1944 IX Troop Carrier Command shoulder patch, locally embroidered in silver bullion, sewn on the right sleeve of Lieutenant Kiesling's jacket.

Close-up of Lieutenant Kiesling's jacket. Note the branch insignia (winged propeller) common to all Airforce officers. Below, the pilot's wings and the ribbon bar: Air Medal, European-African-Middle Eastern Campaign medal (a star denotes participation in a campaign, the arrowhead an airborne assault), Army of Occupation Medal.

113

AMERICAN MILITARY DECORATIONS

1. **Medal of Honor.** Instituted in 1862, it is the highest military decoration in the American Army. It is awarded for 'Extraordinary courage and devotion to duty at the risk of one's life, beyond the call of duty.' Only 294 were awarded during the Second World War. Lt. Col. Cole of the 3rd Battalion, 502nd Regiment, 101st Airborne was awarded the Medal of Honor for leading a bayonet charge over the River Douve bridge at Carentan on 10 June 1944.
2. **Distinguished Service Cross.** Introduced in 1918, it is awarded for exceptional courage in wartime against an enemy of the United States. 4,696 were awarded during the conflict.
3. **Silver Star.** Instituted in 1932, it is awarded for exceptional courage in action against an enemy of the United States.
4. **Bronze Star.** Authorized on 4 February 1944, it is awarded for a valorous behavior in combat.
5. **Distinguished Flying Cross.** Instituted in 1926, it is awarded to personnel of the Army Air Forces for heroism during a war mission. It can also be awarded after a certain number of operational missions against the enemy.
6. **Air Medal.** Introduced on 11 May 1942, it is awarded to flying personnel for a courageous behavior during war missions or for meritorious service, also after a certain number of operational missions.
7. **Purple Heart.** It is awarded for wounds received in combat or in service, it is also awarded posthumously to soldiers killed in combat or to those who died from their wounds. The violet color of the ribbon represents sadness and suffering, the white edge represents relief.

(Henri-Paul Enjames Collection, GI Collector Guide)

Medal of Honor

Distinguished Flying Cross

Silver Star

Bronze Star

Purple Heart

Air Medal

Distinguished Service Cross

European-African-Middle Eastern Campaign Medal.
A star for each campaign, an arrowhead for each amphibious or airborne assault.

Distinguished Unit Citation
Instituted on 26 February 1942.
It is awarded collectively to the personnel of a unit for exceptional behavior in battle.

RIBBON BARS
(See also previous page)

In the courtyard of the Château of Broqueboeuf (La Haye-du-Puits), General Omar N. Bradley, commanding the 1st US Army, decorates several soldiers with the Distinguished Service Crosss. The recipient leaning on a stick is the Lieutenant-Colonel B.H. Vandervoort, commanding the 2/505th PIR (82d A/B div.). His name has been stenciled over the top left-hand pocket of his jacket; strangely, his rank silver oak leaves are pinned on the collar. On his right id Lt. Col. Krause (3/505th Rgt, 82d A/B div.). Note the tightening straps on the trouser pockets of the three officers on the left.
The medic in the center, whom the Geneva Convention forbade to carry a weapon, has been issued with a standard M1 helmet with the early fibre liner. Shod with jump boots, the two paratroopers on the right have changed into new wool trousers and shirt for the ceremony, their jump suits probably having been torn to shreds in combat. Their helmets have got rank insignia on the front. On Vandervoort's left, Captain Rae of the 507th PIR is about to be decorated for leading the attack on the La Fière bridge on 9 June. He is wearing a 'Rigger-Made' pouch containing two grenades. On the right of the photograph, Private Marcus Heim (505th PIR) is about to be awarded the DSC for taking part in the destruction of three tanks with his bazooka on the la Fière bridge on 6 June 1944.
(National Archives)

Captain Benjamin Z. Houston

A Famous Forebear

Capt. Benjamin Houston came down from Samuel Houston (1793-1863), an officer and politician who played an important part in the fair treatment of the American Indians, then in the Independence of Texas, and the war against the Mexicans in 1836. A regular army officer, Benjamin Zachariah Houston was a 2d Lieutenant when he obtained his paratrooper's wings on 17 April 1942. In June 1944 he was a captain, a liaison officer in the 82nd A/B. For his action during an offensive in Normandy on 19 June, he was awarded the Bronze Star. Houston ended his career in 1955 after 20 years and six months' service, with the rank of Major.

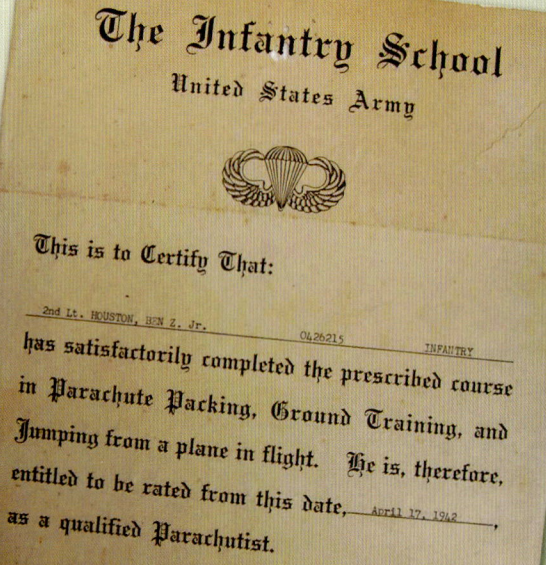

Above, center.
An early-war picture of B. Houston, who wears the parachute infantry round patch on the left side of his garrison cap.

1. Parachute Qualification diploma awarded to 2nd Lieutenant Houston, dated 17 April 1942.
2. 2nd Lieutenant's bars.
3. Captain bars.
4. Bronze Star (medal).
5. Bronze Star (ribbon).
6. Citation for the award of the Bronze Star to Captain Houston.
7. and 8. Paratrooper's wings (front and back).

(Private collection)

CHAPTER 11 THE AIRBORNE DIVISION'S VEHICLES

Because of the limited air-lifting means, the pool of divisional transport vehicles was reduced to just five types: jeep, weapons carrier, Command & recon. Car, Ambulance and GMC truck.

Like the majority of American military vehicles, all these vehicles had four- or six-wheel drive and their mechanical parts were to a great extent standardized.

Apart from the jeeps which were air-transportable (by Waco or Horsa gliders), all the other vehicles were brought in by sea.

Above.
'But where on earth are your infantry?' the German officers asked their American opposite numbers. The American Army was indeed heavily motorized. After dawn on 6 June, the first gliders started bringing in jeeps. The vehicle shown here bears the markings of the 507th PIR, 82d division.
(Reconstruction)

Right.
Passing through Carentan, these two jeeps (the censor has painted over out the tactical markings on the negative) have been assigned different tasks. The first, transporting medics and stretchers, belongs to a medical unit. The second, towing a 57-mm anti-tank gun M1, probably belongs to the 81st AAABn.
(National Archives)

Truck, 1/4-Ton, 4 X 4, "Jeep"

Engine: petrol 4-cylinder, 2 200 cc
Gearbox: 3 forward gears and one reverse. Transfer box, four-wheel drive.
Weight: 3 245 lb.
Max. speed: 55 mph.
Fuel Consumption: 18.7 mpg (miles per gallon)
Purpose: reconnaissance, liaison, command. Could be adapted to carry stretchers.
Scale of issue: 13 in each PIR and 18 in each GIR.

Truck, 3/4-Ton. 4 X 4. Ambulance. Dodge T.214-WC54

Engine: 6-cylinder, 3.8 litre, Dodge T.214 petrol.
Gearbox: Four forward and one reverse gears.
Weight: 7,405 lbs
Fuel Consumption: 9.8 mpg

Truck, 3/4-Ton. 4 X 4, Command (Dodge T.214- WC57)

Engine: 6-cylinder, 3.8 litre, Dodge T.214 petrol.
Gearbox: Four forward and one reverse gears. Transfer box. 4-wheel drive
Weight: 7,158 lbs
Fuel Consumption: 9.4 mpg
Purpose: Command vehicle with radio equipment.

Truck, 3/4-Ton, 4 X 4 (Dodge T.214-WC52)

Engine: 6-cylinder, 3.8 litre, 90 bhp Dodge T.214 petrol.
Gearbox: Four forward and one reverse gears.
Weight: 7,033 lbs
Fuel Consumption: 9.4 mpg.
Purpose: weapons carrier

Truck 2 1/2-Ton, 6 X 6 (GMC CCKW.353)

Engine: 6-cylinder, 4.4 l, General Motors petrol.
Gearbox: 5-speed with overdrive + transfer box. 6-wheel drive
Weight: 15,180 lbs
Fuel consumption: 7.25 mpg
Purpose: transport of personnel and equipment.
Scale of issue: 16 in each PIR and 10 in each GIR.

Cart, Hand, M3A4

This light infantry cart was very much used by the airborne troops and was in service with the PIRs, the GIRs and the Engineer Battalions. It was used to carry all types of loads (equipment, ammunition, machine guns, mortars, etc.) and was drawn by one man or several, or by a vehicle.

Motorcycle, Solo, 45 cu. in. Harley Davidson WLA

Engine: Air-cooled, four stroke, 735 cc, 2-cylinder Vee.
Gearbox: 3-speed with chain transmission.
Weight: 550 lb.
Fuel Consumption: 43 mpg.
Purpose: liaison, traffic control, Military Police.

Scooter, Motor, Airborne (Cushman 53 Autoglide)

Engine: One cylinder 4.5 bhp air-cooled petrol.
Gearbox: two-speed box with chain transmission. Mechanical brake on rear wheel only.
Weight: 253 lb.
Purpose: Liaison, towing the 75-mm pack howitzer.

Truck, Tank, Water 700 Gal., 2 1/2-ton, 6 x 6 GMC CCKW.353

Engine: 6-cylinder, 4.4 l, petrol.
Gearbox: 5-speed with overdrive and transfer box.
Weight: 15 180 lb.
Fuel consumption: 7.25 mpg.
Purpose: water transport (700 gallons).

Trailer, Water tank, 250 Gal., 1-Ton

Trailer, cargo, 1/4-Ton

Jeep trailer
Payload: 550 lbs.   **All-up weight:** 1,047 lbs

Trailer, cargo, 1-Ton

GMC truck trailer
Payload: 2 200 lb.   **All-up weight:** 3,278 lbs.

119

Airborne Engineers Equipment

One of 'Rommel Asparagus' being dug in by the Germans. These stakes caused a lot of losses among the Allied gliders. One of the bulldozers' missions was to rip up these deadly obstacles.
(ECPAD)

Airborne light bulldozer

Engine: 4-cylinder, Waukesha FC 113.
Gearbox: four forward and one reverse gears.
Weight: 4,136 lb.
Hydraulically operated blade; rear-mounted winch.
Scale of issue: 4 per Airborne Engineer Battalion.

GMC-CCKW353A2. 2,1/2-Ton, 6 X 6 (compressor truck)

Boat, Pneumatic, 6-Ton

L: 19 ft 10 in. W: 6 ft.
Weight: 374 lb.
Payload: 6 tons
Folded into a bag: 2' 11" by 2' 11" by 1' 6".
Fitted out with 7 oars. Inflated in 3 minutes by a compressor on the airborne trailer or a GMC brought in by sea.

Truck, Dump, L.W.B. 2 1/2-Ton, 6 X 6

Dump truck used for transporting earth, sand, gravel, etc.

Vehicle Markings

All American military vehicles bore five types of standard markings:

Recognition signs:

White stars were adopted in 1943 for all Allied vehicles. The size was determined by their position on the vehicle.

Army registration numbers:

This was the order of production as the vehicle came off the assembly line. It was preceded by a figure – or number – a prefix indicating the type of vehicle together with the letters USA. This number was painted on the sides of the engine bonnet.

Trailer: 0
Light truck, command car: 2
Jeep: 20
Truck (GMC): 3
Motorcycle: 6
Ambulance: 7

Tactical markings:

1. Unit type codes:
AB: Airborne
AAA: Anti-aircraft, Anti-Tank
E: Engineer
F: Field Artillery
GI: Glider Infantry
I: Infantry (including paratroopers)
M: Medical
P: Military Police
Q: Quartermaster
S: Signals
HQ: Headquarters
SV: Service (Company/battery)
AT: Anti-Tank companies
X: Divisional Headquarters
– Company/battery/troop letter

A to D for the 1st Battalion (inf. regt.) then E, F, G, H, I, K, L, M (2nd and 3rd battalions).

Together with the divisional and unit numbers, these codes were painted in white on the front and rear bumpers.

Bridge Classification plate:

A yellow disk was positioned on the front right of the body, consisting of a black figure indicating the all-up weight category. This figure had to be equal to or less than the figure mentioned on the signs at the entrance to bridges.

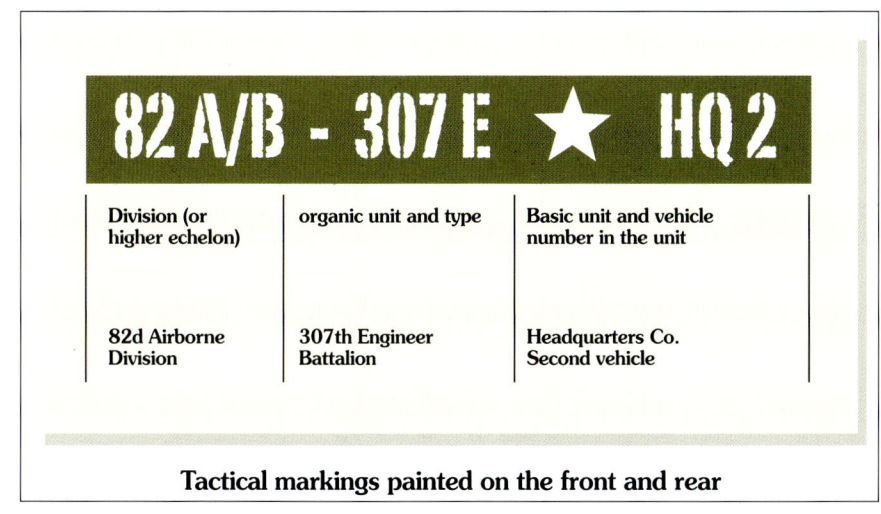

---

82 A/B – 307 E ★ HQ 2

Division (or higher echelon)	organic unit and type	Basic unit and vehicle number in the unit
82d Airborne Division	307th Engineer Battalion	Headquarters Co. Second vehicle

Tactical markings painted on the front and rear

Bridge Classification plate

- 2 — Jeep (15.2 cm)
- 2/2 — Jeep and trailer
- 3 — Dodge (22.9 cm)
- 9/7 — GMC truck and trailer

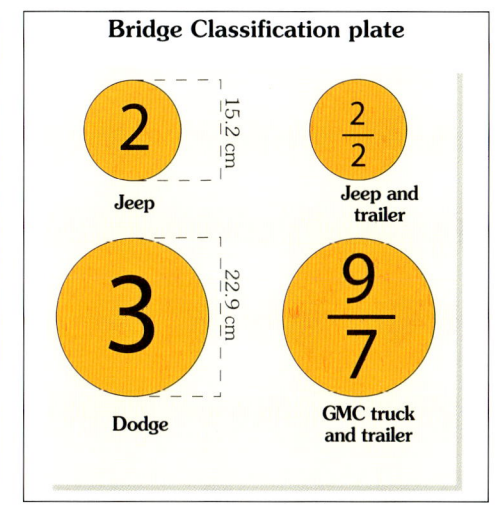

Examples of stenciled markings

ABCDEFGHIJKLMN
OPQRSTUVWXYZ
1234567890

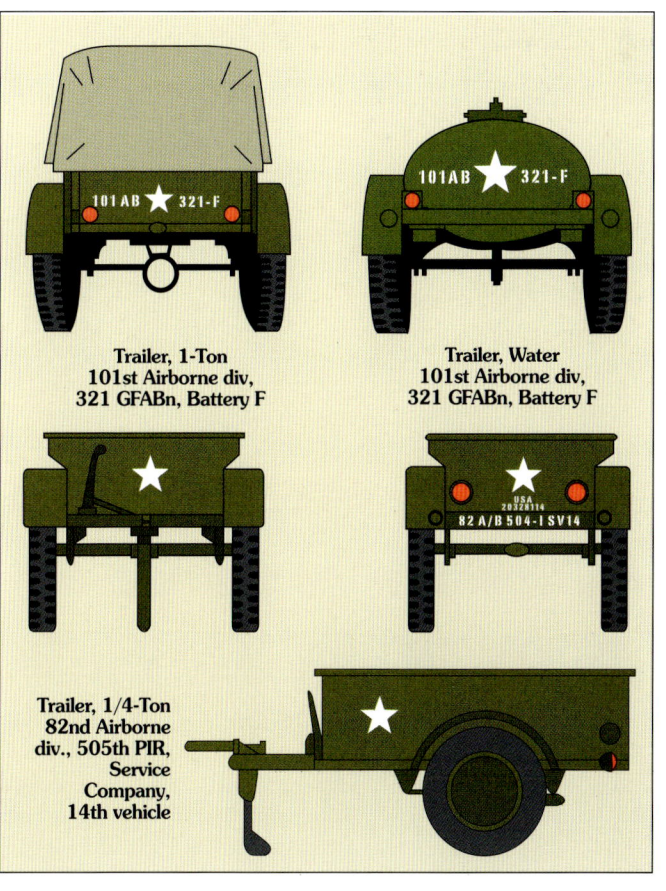

Trailer, 1-Ton
101st Airborne div,
321 GFABn, Battery F

Trailer, Water
101st Airborne div,
321 GFABn, Battery F

Trailer, 1/4-Ton
82nd Airborne div., 505th PIR, Service Company, 14th vehicle

Airplane, liaison, Piper L-4

Power plant: one Lycoming air-cooled 65 bhp flat 4.
Crew: 2.
Max. Speed: 85 mph.
Cruising Speed: 75 mph.
Weight empty: 728 lbs.
Max. take-off weight: 1,216 lbs
Wingspan: 35' 4".
Length: 22' 2". **Height:** 6' 7".
Liaison and artillery observation.

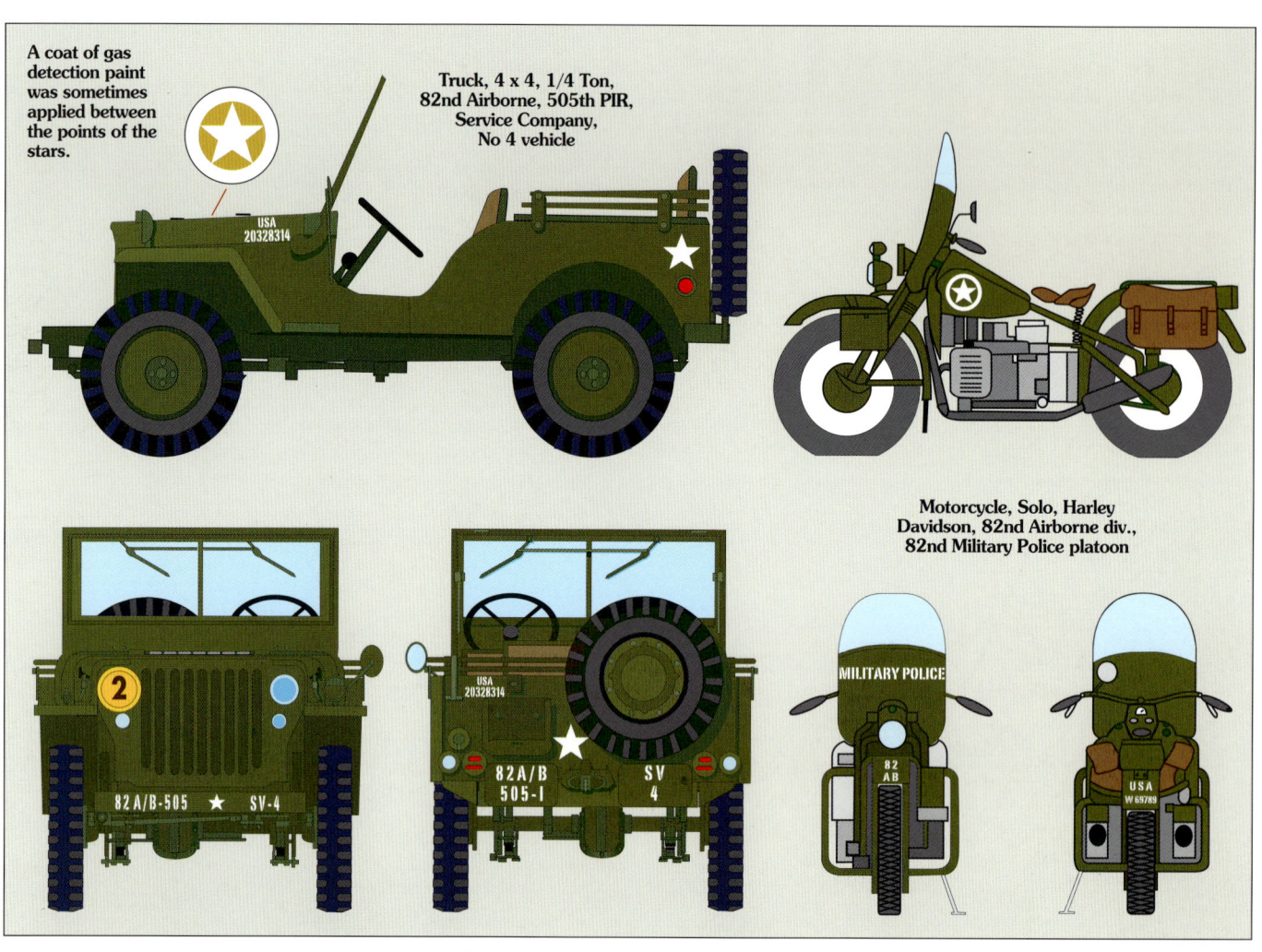

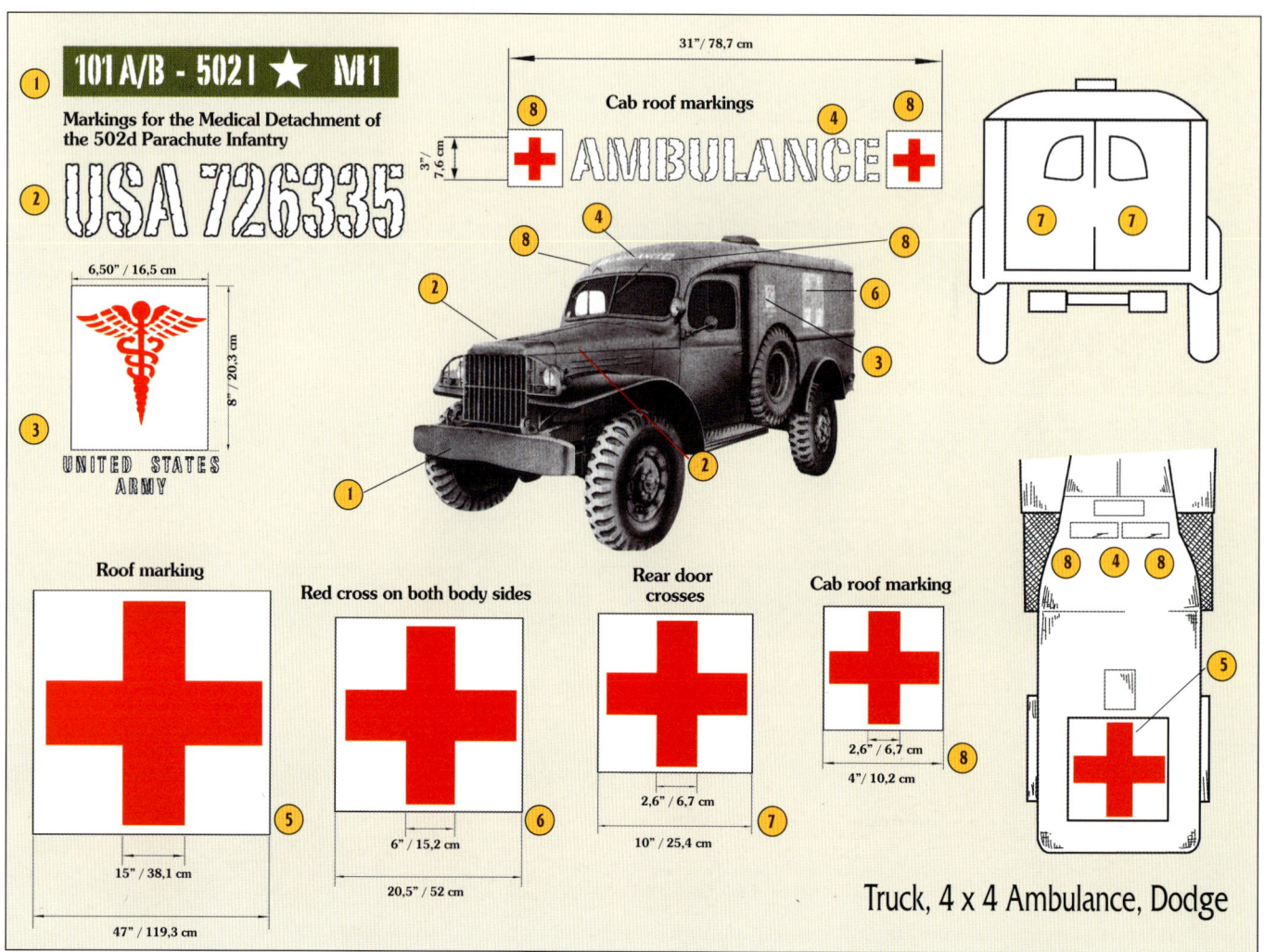

A coat of gas detection paint was sometimes applied between the points of the stars.

Truck, 4 x 4, 1/4 Ton, 82nd Airborne, 505th PIR, Service Company, No 4 vehicle

Motorcycle, Solo, Harley Davidson, 82nd Airborne div., 82nd Military Police platoon

101 A/B - 5021 ★ M1

Markings for the Medical Detachment of the 502d Parachute Infantry

USA 726335

6,50" / 16,5 cm
8" / 20,3 cm

UNITED STATES ARMY

31" / 78,7 cm
Cab roof markings
3" / 7,6 cm
✚ AMBULANCE ✚

Roof marking
15" / 38,1 cm
47" / 119,3 cm

Red cross on both body sides
6" / 15,2 cm
20,5" / 52 cm

Rear door crosses
2,6" / 6,7 cm
10" / 25,4 cm

Cab roof marking
2,6" / 6,7 cm
4" / 10,2 cm

Truck, 4 x 4 Ambulance, Dodge

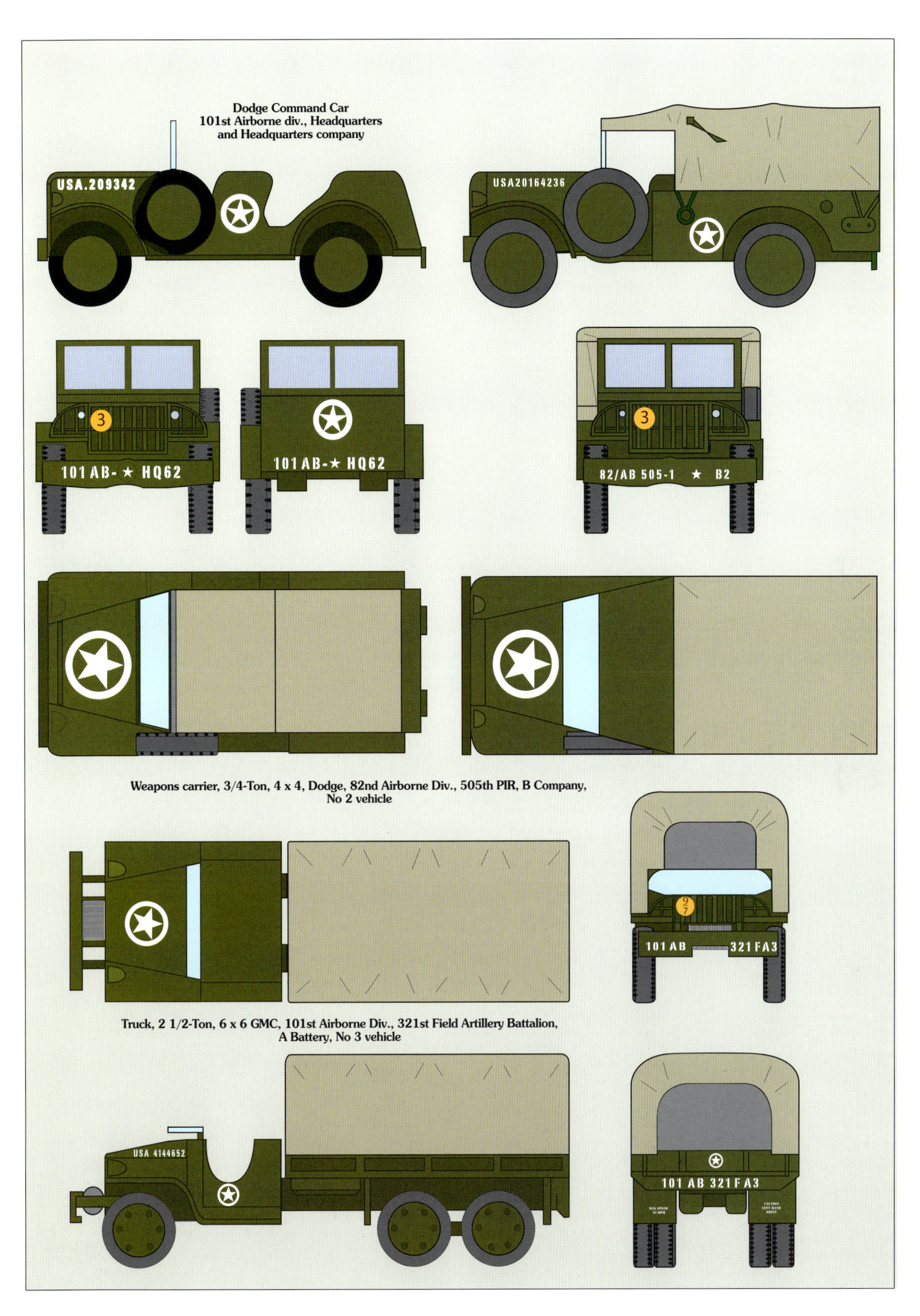

Dodge Command Car
101st Airborne div., Headquarters and Headquarters company

Weapons carrier, 3/4-Ton, 4 x 4, Dodge, 82nd Airborne Div., 505th PIR, B Company, No 2 vehicle

Truck, 2 1/2-Ton, 6 x 6 GMC, 101st Airborne Div., 321st Field Artillery Battalion, A Battery, No 3 vehicle

APPENDIX 1
PRISONERS AND STRAGGLERS

Fighting on D-Day did not always take place under humane conditions, as the adjoining photos would lead us to believe.

Above.
This aging German soldier, scarcely a firebrand, obligingly raises his arms in front of the Associated Press photographer's camera. This shot enables us to see the large strips of felt under this 101st Airborne div. paratrooper's belt suspenders and his many trophies (fiber canteen, stick grenades, bayonet). The GI at the rear is equipped with the assault jacket also worn by Rangers and first-wave units on D-day. It seems that this item was issued to a small number of Glider-borne soldiers.

Above.
**July 1944: the muddled marking-out of the drop zones, the darkness, the clouds and the fog were responsible for of a lot of the sticks getting dispersed. Dropped a long way behind enemy lines, Sergeants Robert D. Henderson and Havrill W. Lazenby from the 505th PIR (82nd A/B div.) took 37 days to join up with their unit. Henderson is armed with a German k98 rifle, th leather belt and buckle are also captured items.
Lazenby is armed with a Gewehr 41 semi-auto rifle and has hooked part of a German cartridge pocket on his breast pocket. Both have made themselves a scarf from camouflaged parachute cloth.**
(National Archives)

Caught up in the infernal spiral of the fighting, often hand-to-hand, the combatants from both sides did not give quarter. American paratroopers, who had landed on the top of tall trees and tried desperately to get themselves untangled from their parachute harness, were shot like sitting ducks.

At Graignes, eight paratroopers who had been dropped 12 miles from their objective were captured and executed in cold blood near the Mesnil-Angot hamlet. French civilians discovered their bodies under a thin layer of earth.

Previous page.
**In a POW cage at Tessy-sur-Vire, near Saint-Lô, these American airborne officers watch incoming flights of Allied planes. The Captain in the foreground is curiously enough wearing a field jacket matched to paratrooper trousers.
The officer in the center with his hands in his pockets is a glider pilot. He has standard wool trousers with leggings and service shoes. The man on the left who is rubbing his nose is a parachute artilleryman whose insignia can be seen on the shirt: crossed cannons on the collar and paratrooper wings above the left breast pocket. On the far right, the officer wearing glasses has a USAAF A-2 leather flying jacket, that was commonly worn by paratrooper officers.**
(ECPAD)

Right.
**This young paratrooper - some of them were only eighteen - is being interrogated by a German interpreter. According to the international conventions, the prisoner could only indicate his age, rank and serial number.
Under his jump trousers with Air Force braces, he wears for warmth the regular wool serge trousers.**
(ECPAD)

125

Exeter, 5 June 1944.
The 'Lady Lillian' was a C-47 from HQ Squadron, 440th TCG, piloted by First-Lieutenant Luoma. He flew in a stick, No2 from the HQ Co. 3/506th PIR, 101st AB division, led by Lt Bobuck. Luoma took off at 23.50 and reached DZ 'D' (Angoville-au-Plain) at 01.45.
(Computer artwork by Nicolas Gohin, © Histoire & Collections 2004)

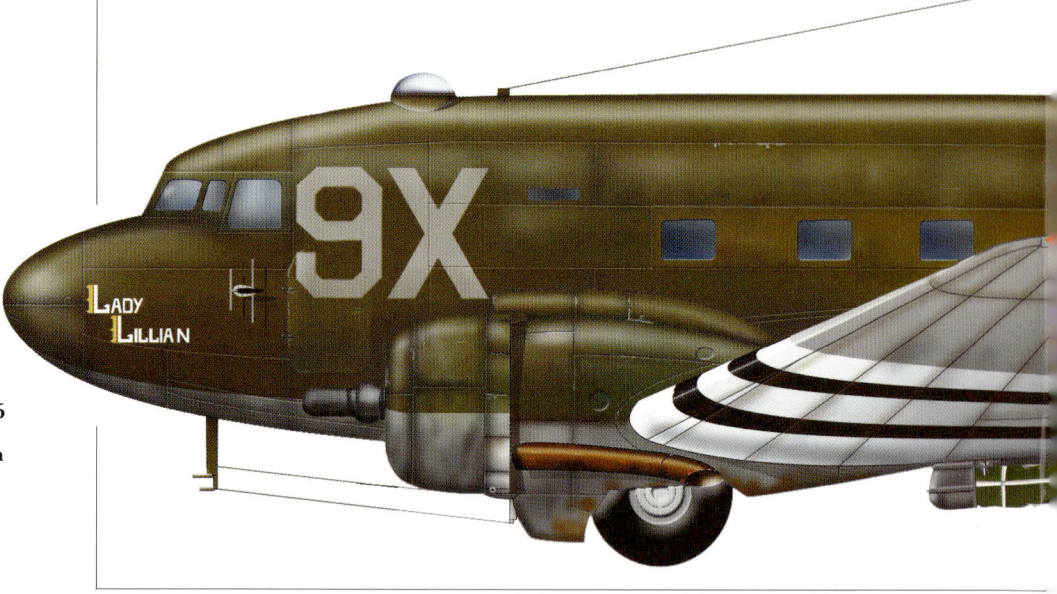

Below.
Lt Bobuck's second stick, from the 3/506 PIR, 101st AB division, inside the cabin of the C-47 'Lady Lillian' (shown above) a few moments before taking off for Normandy. In the left-hand row, the second paratrooper from the rear is Technician 5th Grade William H. Atlee who was killed on 6 June 1944 and whose helmet is shown on page 59.

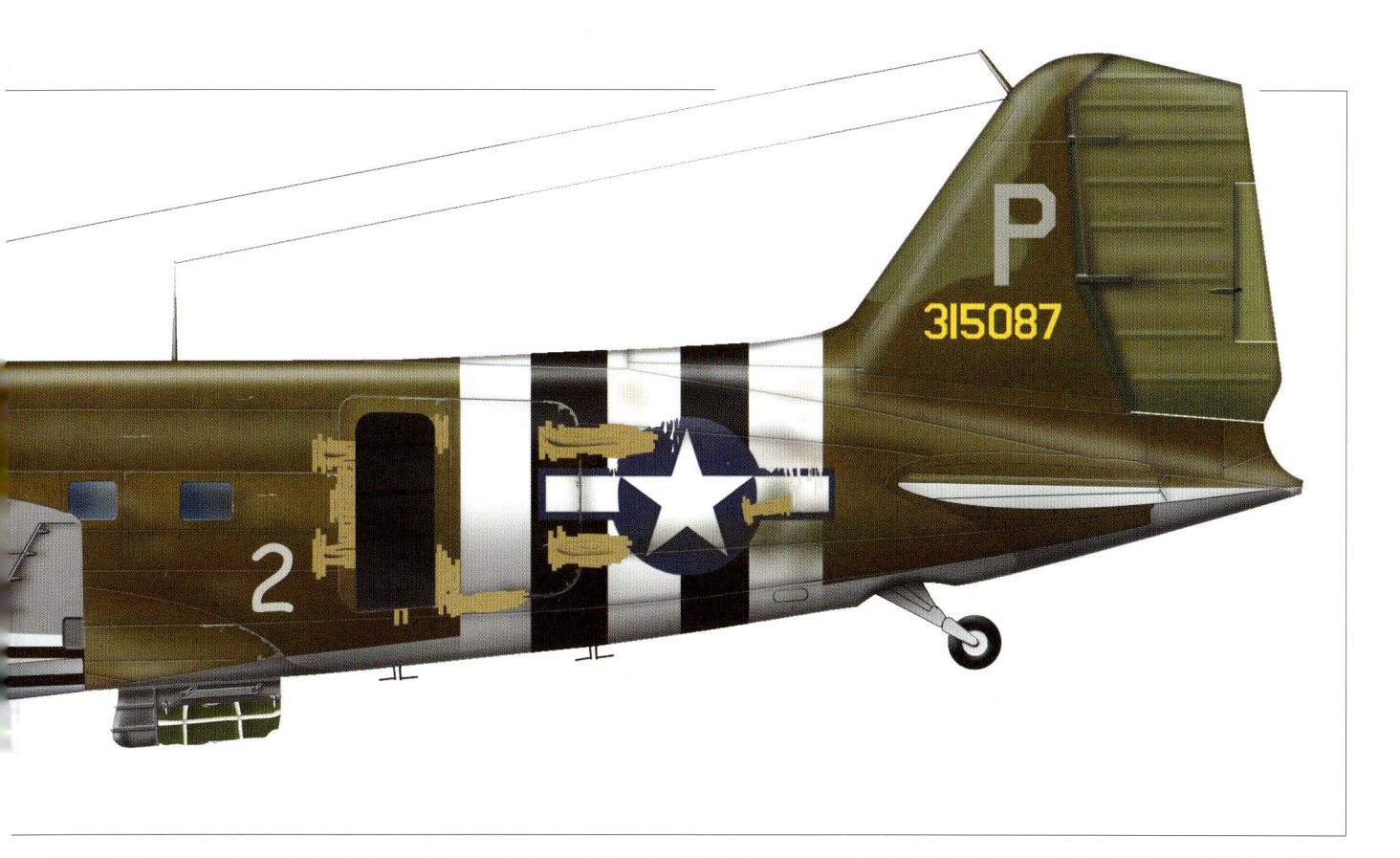

APPENDIX 2   AIRBORNE DIVISION ARTILLERY

Gun, Anti Tank, 57-mm, M1

British design (6-Pdr A/T gun)
Split trail carriage, drawn by jeep.
Flown-in by Waco or Horsa glider
Total weight: 2 640 lb
Shell weight: 6 lb 4 oz
Average range: 625 yards
Muzzle velocity: 907 yards/s.
Piercing capability:
3.3 inches at an angle of 30° (APCBP projectile).
Rate of fire: 15 rounds per minute
Gun crew: 4 or 5
Scale of issue: Divisional Airborne Anti-aircraft Battalion

75-mm Pack Howitzer M1A1, Carriage M8

Caliber: 75-mm
Total weight: 1 320 lb
Shell weight: 14 lb
Max. range: 5 1/3 miles
Rate of fire: 6 rounds/mn
Set up time: 3 minutes
Articulated single trail, towed by jeep or Dodge.
Note: the howitzer could be dismantled and dropped by plane in 7 containers or brought-in already assembled by glider.
Scale of issue: PFABns and GFABns.

Because of the difficulties in flying equipment in, the airborne artillery battalions were reduced to using two types of guns: the light 75-mm pack howitzer and the 57-mm anti-tank gun.
(National Archives)

127

ACKNOWLEDGEMENTS

This study would not have been possible without the help and cooperation of several museums
and private collectors as well as the support of many friends.
Heartfelt thanks to them are expressed here.
To our friend Jean Bouchery for his invaluable help;
Pierre Besnard who put his unique collection of US Army insignia and his large collection of documents
on the Troop Carriers at our disposal;
Philippe Charbonnier, editor of 'Militaria Magazine' for his technical assistance;
Henri-Paul Enjames for graciously letting us use illustrations from his book *'GI Collector's Guide, US Army Theater of Operations,*
published by Histoire & Collections in 2003;
Our Norman friend for lending his invaluable collection of items from the battlefield, his generous welcome and his helpfulness.
We would also like to thank: Denis, Eric, Véronique Barbe, Maurice Bazin, Patrice Bouchery, the ubiquitous Laurent Charbonneau,
as well as:
Alain Dodat (†), Jean-Michel Denis, Frédéric Finel, Denis Gandilhon, Jon Gawne for photo research at the National Archives in
Washington DC, Didier and Pascal Lodieu, Le Cap, Yann Le Vu, Eric Miquelon, Jean-Yves Nasse, Bertrand Paris, Pierre Schubert, Yves
Tariel, Christian Tollet, Joël Tomadesso, Daniel Treffeu, and the 'Club Saint-Maur.'
We would also like to thanks the curators of the following museums:
– Musée de la Second Guerre Mondiale (WWII Museum) at Ambleteuse, CD 940, 62164 Ambleteuse (Pas-de-Calais)
Website: www.musee3945.com
– Musée Mémorial d'Omaha Beach, Les Moulins, Rue de la Mer, 14710 St-Laurent-sur-Mer.
– Musée de la Percée d'Avranches, le Moulinet, Le Val Saint-Pierre, 50300 Avranches,
and finally these two excellent militaria shops in Paris:
'Le Poilu,' 18, rue Emile Duclaux, 75015 Paris, France.
'Overlord,' 96 rue de la Folie Méricourt; 75011, Paris, France.

BIBLIOGRAPHY

**A number of books have been devoted to the story of the US Airborne on 6 June 1944, as well as the plight of the French population
caught up in the maelstrom of the battle, which has been rarely depicted in recent movies.
To find out why, read *'Parachutés sur Sainte-Mère-Eglise,'* by Albert Pipet.
Some of these books, published in the immediate post-war years, were first-hand eye-witness accounts and were used as additional reference for this study. Several, however mentioned in the list below, are nowadays out of print, but the history buff must not be discouraged: they can still be found if one looks patiently through the specialised and second-hand bookshops.**

— *At the point of no return,* Michel de Trez, D-Day Publishing, 1994
— *American Warriors,* Michel de Trez, D-Day Publishing, 1994
— *American Airborne Pathfinders in WW II,* Jeff Moran, Schiffer Military History, 2003
— *Les paras US de Normandie,* Jean Bouchery and Christophe Deschodt, Militaria Magazine n° 22/23
— *101st Airborne,* Mark Bando, MBI Publishing, 2001
— *Pulse and repulse,* Rex Shana, Eakin Press, 1995
— *Green lights,* Martin Wolfe, University of Pennsylvania Press, 1989
— *Un pont en Normandie,* Gilles Bré, 2003
— *DZ Europe, the story of the 440th Troop Carrier Group*
— *Objectif Sainte-Mère-Église,* Éditions Heimdal.

— *Jour J,* Éditions Heimdal.
— *Les paras US.* H.J. Renaud, L. Mari, G. Bernage, P. Lejuée. Éditions Heimdal.
— *Airborne Album.* John C. Andrews. H & Pelz.

— USAAF Illustrated catalog, September 1943
— *Air Force in WW II,* Ken C. Rust, Aero Publishers, 1970
— *Le Dakota,* Jacques Borgé and Nicolas Viasnoff, EPA 1980
— *L'histoire du Douglas DC 3.* Yves Tariel. 1985.
— *Parachute Test Platoon to Normandy.* John C. Andrews.
— *Les planeurs américains.* P. Esvelin. Éditions Heimdal.
— *WW II Allied gliders,* ISO publication, 1987
— *WW II Gliders pilots,* Turner Publishing, 1991
— *D-Day Gliders, les planeurs américains du Jour-J,* Philippe Esvelin, Heimdal, 2001

— Order of Battle, Utah beach and the US Airborne divisions, James and Roberta Wiener, Ravelin Limited, 1994
— *US Army 1944-1945, Marquages et organisation.* E. Becker et J. Milmeister.
— Order of battle, US Army WW II. Shelby L. Stanton.
— United States Army Ground Forces, tables of organization and equipment. J.-J. Hays.
— *U.S. Army Handbook 1941-1945.* George Forty.
— Quartermaster Supply Catalog. August 1943.
— Quartermaster Corps Historical studies. 1944-1946.

— *The M1 Helmet,* Mark A. Reynosa, Schiffer Military History, 1996
— *Steel pots,* Chris Arnold, James Bender Publishing, 1997
— *US Combat Helmets of the 20th century,* Mark A. Reynosa, Schiffer Military History, 1997

— *Paratrooper!,* G.M. Devlin. 1979.
— *Parachutés sur Sainte-Mère-Église.* Albert Pipet. 1984.
— *L'invasion aéroportée en Normandie.* S.L.A. Marshall 1968.
— *Les paras US dans le canton de Sainte-Mère-Église.* P. Jutras. 1979.
— *Saut dans l'obscurité.* Thomas W. Porcella. 1986.
— *La brèche de Sainte-Marie du Mont.* François Lemonier. Gruhier. 1965.
— *Les chemins de l'été 1944.* Albert Desile. 1983.
— *Sainte-Mère-Église.* Alexandre Renaud. 1955.

— *Utah Beach to Cherbourg.* American Forces in Action Series. The Battery Press. Nashville. 1947.
— *Cross Channel Attack.* G. Harrison. US Army in WW II series, GPO Wash. DC.